Cambridge Elements

Elements in the History and Politics of Fascism
edited by
Federico Finchelstein
The New School for Social Research
António Costa Pinto
University of Lisbon

THE FASCIST ZENITH

War and Dictatorship under Axis Rule

António Costa Pinto
University of Lisbon

Shaftesbury Road, Cambridge CB2 8EA, United Kingdom

One Liberty Plaza, 20th Floor, New York, NY 10006, USA

477 Williamstown Road, Port Melbourne, VIC 3207, Australia

314–321, 3rd Floor, Plot 3, Splendor Forum, Jasola District Centre, New Delhi – 110025, India

103 Penang Road, #05–06/07, Visioncrest Commercial, Singapore 238467

Cambridge University Press is part of Cambridge University Press & Assessment, a department of the University of Cambridge.

We share the University's mission to contribute to society through the pursuit of education, learning and research at the highest international levels of excellence.

www.cambridge.org
Information on this title: www.cambridge.org/9781009706681

DOI: 10.1017/9781009706674

© António Costa Pinto 2025

This publication is in copyright. Subject to statutory exception and to the provisions of relevant collective licensing agreements, no reproduction of any part may take place without the written permission of Cambridge University Press & Assessment.

When citing this work, please include a reference to the DOI 10.1017/9781009706674

First published 2025

A catalogue record for this publication is available from the British Library

ISBN 978-1-009-70666-7 Hardback
ISBN 978-1-009-70668-1 Paperback
ISSN 2977-0416 (online)
ISSN 2977-0408 (print)

Cambridge University Press & Assessment has no responsibility for the persistence or accuracy of URLs for external or third-party internet websites referred to in this publication and does not guarantee that any content on such websites is, or will remain, accurate or appropriate.

For EU product safety concerns, contact us at Calle de José Abascal, 56, 1°, 28003 Madrid, Spain, or email eugpsr@cambridge.org

The Fascist Zenith

War and Dictatorship under Axis Rule

Elements in the History and Politics of Fascism

DOI: 10.1017/9781009706674
First published online: November 2025

António Costa Pinto
University of Lisbon
Author for correspondence: António Costa Pinto, acpinto@ics.ulisboa.pt

Abstract: The year 1942 represents the apex of the global wave of autocratization associated with the Era of Fascism and the expansion of Axis rule during World War II, which were responsible for this impressive growth of authoritarian "occupation" regimes. Starting in Asia with the imperialist expansion of Japan, followed by Nazi Germany and Fascist Italy in Europe, the number of dictatorships increased substantially. This Element analyzes how the three poles of Axis rule, Fascist Italy, Nazi Germany, and Authoritarian Japan, led the dynamics of institution-building of political regimes of occupation under their direct or indirect control, respective diffusion models, and, in some cases, coercive transfers.

Keywords: fascism, World War II, dictatorship, military occupation, Axis

© António Costa Pinto 2025

ISBNs: 9781009706667 (HB), 9781009706681 (PB), 9781009706674 (OC)
ISSNs: 2977-0416 (online), 2977-0408 (print)

Contents

Introduction   1

1 Diffusion, Coercion, and the Building of Political Regimes under Axis Rule   4

2 Italian Fascism in the Balkans: Exporting Fascist Institutions   8

3 Nazi Germany: A "Patchwork" of Dictatorships and Quasi-governments Blinking at Regimes   16

4 Japan's "Greater East Asia Co-Prosperity Sphere" and Its Occupation Regimes   48

5 Making States and Regimes under Axis Rule: Concluding Remarks   69

Select Bibliography   84

Introduction

The purpose of this Element is to analyze how the three poles of Axis rule, Nazi Germany, Fascist Italy, and Authoritarian Japan, led the dynamics of institution-building of political regimes of occupation under their direct or indirect control.[1] The Axis powers were characterized by different models and varied tensions and forced compromises between native elites of different extractions, namely conservative, fascist, radical-right, and nationalist movements and elites, with the occupier far from being a political actor with a unified strategy of regime promotion. Military occupation represents the highest degree of political, social, and economic control over an occupied state and its society, "opening the possibility of installing political structures or procedures that can guarantee mid-range influence on the regime's character."[2] However, even if it always gives rise to an "authoritarian situation" with its cohort of repression and economic exploitation, the nature of direct or indirect military occupation is diverse in strategy and type, giving rise in some cases to dictatorial political regimes. We can define military occupation as "the temporary control of a territory by a state (or group of allied states) that makes no claim to permanent sovereignty over that territory," indicating, as David M. Edelstein has noticed, a critical distinction from annexation or colonialism.[3] This definition is particularly useful in a war juncture such as World War II, where military occupation sometimes far exceeded the imperialistic strategic projects of Axis powers, forcing them to occupy territories based on unforeseen developments in the war. Nevertheless, occupation always requires some form of administration by specific branches of the occupying forces, usually military and civilian in different proportions.

The decision to build an occupation state, that is, "a political regime installed to administer occupied territory in the interests of the occupying power,"[4] is always one among several options available for the occupying power. The dynamics of the military occupations of Axis powers illustrates this diversity quite well, from the creation of political regimes,

---

[1] See António Costa Pinto and Goffredo Adinolfi, eds., *Building Dictatorships under Axis Rule: War, Military Occupation and Political Regimes*, London, Routledge, 2025.
[2] M. Kneuer and T. Demmelhuber, "Conceptualizing authoritarian gravity centers: Sources and addressees, mechanisms and motives of authoritarian pressure and attraction," in M. Kneuer and T. Demmelhuber, eds., *Authoritarian Gravity Centers: A Cross-Regional Study of Authoritarian Promotion and Diffusion*, London, Routledge, 2021, p. 12.
[3] See David M. Edelstein, *Occupational Hazards: Success and Failure in Military Occupation*, Ithaca, NY, Cornell University Press, 2008, pp. 3–4.
[4] Timothy Brook, *Collaborating: Japanese Agents and Local Elites in Wartime China*, Cambridge, MA, Harvard University Press, 2005, pp. 12–13.

such as the "French State," the "Slovak State," Albania, Manchukuo, or "The State of Burma," to direct military administration in Belgium and Java, and hesitations between the creation of a fascist occupation regime led by Vidkun Quisling or the maintaining of the Reichskommissar model in Norway (Table 1, Table 2).

Table 1 Political Administration of Selected Occupied Territories under Axis Rule in Europe

Dominant power	Country or region	Period	Occupation regime
Italy Germany	Albania	1939–43	Protectorate ("Kingdom of Albania in personal union with Italy")
		1943–44	Independent State ("Kingdom of Albania")
Germany	Belgium	1940–44	Military Administration
		1944–45	Reichskommissariat
Germany	Bohemia and Moravia	1939–45	Protectorate of Bohemia and Moravia
Italy-Germany	Croatia	1941–45	Independent State ("Independent State of Croatia")
Germany	Denmark	1940–45	Independent State
Germany	Estonia	1941–44	Reichskommissariat
Germany-Italy	France	1940–45	Independent State ("French State")
Italy-Germany	Greece	1941–44	Military Administration
Germany	Hungary	1940–44	Independent State ("Kingdom of Hungary")
		1944–45	"Government of National Union"
Germany	Italy	1943–45	Independent State ("Italian Social Republic")
Germany	Latvia	1941–45	Reichskommissariat
Germany	Lithuania	1941–45	Reichskommissariat
Germany	Netherlands	1940–45	Reichskommissariat
Germany	Norway	1940–45	Reichskommissariat
Germany	Serbia	1941–44	Military Administration
Germany	Slovakia	1939–45	Independent State ("Slovak State")

Source: Created by the author.

Table 2 Political Administration of Selected Occupied Territories under Axis Rule in Asia

Dominant power	Country or region	Period	Occupation regime
Japan	Burma	1942–45	Independent State ("State of Burma")
Japan	China	1932–34	Independent State ("State of Manchuria, Manchukuo")
		1934–45	Independent State ("Empire of [Great] Manchuria")
Japan	China	1940–45	Independent State ("Reorganized National Government of the Republic of China")
Japan	Java	1942–45	Military Administration
Japan	Philippines	1942–45	Independent State ("Second Philippine Republic")
Japan	Thailand	1941–45	Independent State ("Kingdom of Thailand")

Source: Created by the author.

As Ian T. Gross wrote, "setting up a collaborationists' regime in an occupied country requires ... first of all, that a major political decision be made by the occupier,"[5] but there too, if some Axis Powers had a more unitarian decision-making process, as in Fascist Italy, in others, like Nazi Germany and in a way Imperial Japan, the process was more complex. In Germany, the regime's decision-making process added complexity and the initial move toward the creation of the State of Manchukuo, for example, was legitimated by Tokyo some months after the decision of the Kwuantung Army to occupy Manchuria. Another dimension to be considered, since it was very much present during World War II, was simply the contingency of some unpredictable military occupation processes, like the German occupation of Greece, after the initial failure of Fascist Italy, giving place to a collaborationist government that did not create a new political regime. The example could be extended to several cases of Japan's military occupation in Asia as well.

This Element examines how the complicated ideological, political, and economic relationship between the occupying forces and different segments

---

[5] Jan T. Gross, *Polish Society under German Occupation: The Generalgouvernement, 1939–1944*, Princeton, NJ, Princeton University Press, 1979, p. 131.

of national and sub-national elites were present in the institutional crafting of new regimes. Military occupation opened in some cases a window of opportunity for the takeover of power by different segments of these authoritarian elites, and the tension and forced pacts between different projects of institutionalization of dictatorships were clear signs of this dynamic process. In this context, the debates and the praxis of the construction of new dictatorships are analyzed, so that we can identify the design of their institutions, the segments of the political elites that hegemonize them, the diffusion, promotion and conditionality of models present, and the attitudes of the Axis powers before them.

1 Diffusion, Coercion, and the Building of Political Regimes under Axis Rule

The interwar period, as Kurt Weyland wrote, was characterized on the right of the political spectrum by "a division between most established elites, who preferred conservative, top-down, non-mobilizational authoritarianism, and charismatic upstart leaders and their fervent, violent mass followers, who spearheaded a dynamic bottom-up push for mobilizational, fascist totalitarianism."[6] This dynamic crosses almost all the dictatorships associated with the Era of Fascism, from Latin America to Japan, and when examining new authoritarian political institutions and models under Axis rule, it is also very much present, with a different mix of fascist, conservative, radical-right, and nationalist winners and losers.

The models most often mentioned during the late 1930s of new authoritarian political institutions typical of the Era of Fascism were the Italian Fascist regime and German National Socialism. With personalized leadership, corporatist political representation as an alternative to liberal parliamentarism, and the single party as the three main institutional features of the new fascist-era dictatorships, few looked at Nazi Germany when crafting their political institutions.[7] The same cannot be said of Italian Fascism or even of other regimes more sympathetic to the radical right.[8]

---

[6] K. Weyland, *Assault on Democracy: Communism, Fascism and Authoritarianism*, Cambridge, Cambridge University Press, 2021, p. 83.

[7] With the exception of social policy. On the diffusion of National Socialist (NS) social institutions, see S. Kott and K. K. Patel, eds., *Nazism across Borders: The Social Policies of the Third Reich and Their Global Appeal*, Oxford, Oxford University Press, 2018.

[8] See J. Steffek, "Fascist internationalism," *Millenium: Journal of International Studies*, 44 (2015), pp. 3–22; M. Pasetti, *L'Europa Corporativa: Una Storia Transnazionale tra le Due Guerre Mondiali*, Bologna, Bononia University Press, 2016; A. C. Pinto, ed., *An Authoritarian Third Way in the Era of Fascism: Diffusion, Models and Interactions in Europe and Latin America*, London, Routledge, 2022.

Nevertheless, there were many variations, emulation processes, and even regime promotion in various directions during the genuine authoritarian political laboratory of the Era of Fascism.

The three dominant poles of the Axis sketched models of imperialist expansion before World War II and perhaps the most coherent, that is, those whose regime design represented the greatest presence of the respective exported models, were Manchukuo, in the case of Japan, and Albania, in the case of Italian Fascism. The closest model, in the case of National Socialist Germany, would be Austria, but after the Anschluss Austria was purely and simply annexed into the Third Reich.

When Nazi Germany became the dominant power in occupied Europe during the early 1940s, several cultural, social, and especially economic projects for a European "new order" were developed by Nazi institutions, sometimes in collaboration (and some tension) with Fascist Italy. The same happened, in fact in a much more intense way, with Imperial Japan, and its "Greater East Asia Co-Prosperity Sphere."[9] But compared with Fascist Italy and Authoritarian Japan, National Socialism was less consistent in the coercive transfer of a model of regime to be imposed. If economic exploitation was an obvious common denominator, anti-Semitism as an ideological element and praxis of extermination of Jewish communities was perhaps the most coherent and transversally imposed project by Nazi Germany. Fascist Italy and Authoritarian Japan "exported" much more clearly the political institutions they intended to consolidate in their countries, namely in their "model regimes," such as in Albania or Manchukuo. Nevertheless, between pressures from national (and sub-national) collaborationist elites and the diversity of political, economic, and military institutions operating in the field, the Axis policies in Europe and Asia evolved toward a sort of "polycratic fabric of occupations," opening a window of opportunity for the construction of different types of collaborationist dictatorships.[10]

Amid a conjuncture of war and sudden changes in the locus of decision-making of the occupants, these dictatorships did not consolidate themselves. In some cases, their political systems almost did not come into

---

[9] See Mark Mazower, *Hitler's Empire: Nazi Rule in Occupied Europe*, London, Allen Lane, 2008; B. G. Martin, *The Nazi-Fascist New Order for European Culture*, Cambridge, MA, Harvard University Press, 2016; R. Bauer, *The Construction of a National Socialist Europe during the Second World War: How the New Order Took Shape*, London, Routledge, 2020; G.-H. Soutou, *Europa! Les Projects Européens de L'Allemagne Nazie et L'Italie Fasciste*, Paris, Tallandier, 2021.

[10] B. Kundrus, *Krieg und Holocaust in Europa*, Munich, Beck, 2018, p. 149, cited in S. Reichardt, "Fascism's stages: Imperial violence, entanglement and processualization," *Journal of the History of Ideas*, 82 (1) (2021), p. 87.

operation or were blocked and changed by the occupation authorities. However, they left an impressive ballast of legal norms, constitutions, projects, and models of single or dominant parties and institutions regulating state–society relations. The nature of the single party and the model of authoritarian political and social representation they almost all tried to create are further crucial indicators of the institution-building of these dictatorships. From this perspective, the fate of corporatism in authoritarian institution-building under Axis rule is illustrative of the degree of independence and diversity of the national political elites in the institutional design of these regimes and the varied conditionality of the occupying forces.

Italian Fascism and Imperial Japan based their project of political institution building on varieties of corporatism in terms of social and political representation and the single party. Social corporatism offered autocrats a formalized system of interest representation with which to manage the economy and labor relations, legitimizing the repression of free trade unions through the co-optation of some of their groups into state-controlled unions, often with compulsory membership. Social corporatism then became synonymous with the forced unification of organized interests into single units of employers and employees tightly controlled by the state, which ended their independence, especially the independence of the trade unions. During the Era of Fascism, "political corporatism" mainly referred to the comprehensive organization of political society, which sought to replace liberal democracy with "an anti-individualist system of representation based on an 'organic statist' view of society in which its organic units (families, local powers, professional associations and interest organizations and institutions) replace the individual-centered electoral model of representation and parliamentary legitimacy, and thereby becoming the primary and/or complementary legislative or advisory body of the ruler's executive."[11] Although political corporatism by definition only marked "independent" regimes, social corporatism, in the context of an economy of war, became an important institutional device, with an economy controlled by the occupying power, and therefore also marked other types of occupation by the Axis.

Despite being an international and military alliance, the Axis states not only had converging strategic interests in the international arena but

---

[11] A. C. Pinto, *The Nature of Fascism Revisited*, New York: SSM-Columbia University Press, 2012, p. 122; A. C. Pinto, ed., *Corporatism and Fascism: The Corporatist Wave in Europe*, London, Routledge, 2017.

were also regimes that had some common pattern, in terms of political elite culture and institutions from the Era of Fascism. Thus, even though the convergence between its three poles was international, as Christian Goeschel stressed, the Axis introduced "a new aggressive style of global diplomacy heavily focused on mass spectacles of unity and strength. ... This configuration created a dynamic that made the leaders of the regimes, their peoples, but also those on the enemy side believe in the strength of this global pact of three aggressive-militaristic powers."[12] Although fragile and short, this attempt to create an Axis "imagined community" was complemented by a policy of legitimation of "independent states" in military occupied countries and territories, through a dynamic of mutual diplomatic recognition. From this perspective, although in some cases international recognition exceeded the Axis, the latter constituted its hard core, sometimes accompanied by the beginning of cooperation and cultural and political diffusion. This dynamic of mutual recognition of states such as Manchukuo, the "Slovak State," the "Independent State of Croatia," the "State of Burma," or the "Second Philippine Republic" also included, in addition to Germany, Italy, and Japan, other members of Axis such as Hungary, Bulgaria, non-belligerent members, such as Francoist Spain, and even some neutral countries. Endowed with authoritarian political regimes, these dictatorships represented in their variety the apex of the autocratic wave of the Era of Fascism. With this progressive convergence of military alliances, international imperialistic strategy, and, in a more limited way, even ideology, the three poles of the Axis powers developed variants of dictatorial political regimes from the Era of Fascism, and radicalization and war brought them closer together.[13]

This Element deals with the process of institution-building of dictatorships in some countries and regions under German, Italian, and Japanese direct or indirect military occupation and will be structured around three axes: the nature of the political elites of these regimes, the creation of a single or dominant party, and the levels of institutionalization of political and social corporatism, respective diffusion models, and, in some cases,

---

[12] Christian Goeschel, "Performing the new order: The tripartite pact, 1940–1945," *Contemporary European History*, 33 (2024), pp. 411–427. See especially Daniel Hedinger, *Die Achse Berlin-Rom-Tokio 1919–1946*, Munich, CH Beck, 2021.

[13] For the development of Axis rule as empires, see Louise Young, *Japan's Total Empire: Manchuria and the Culture of Wartime Imperialism*, Berkeley, The University of California Press, 1998; D. Rodogno, *Fascism's European Empire: Italian Occupation during the Second World War*, Cambridge, Cambridge University Press, 2006; Mazower, *Hitler's Empire*; S. Baranowski, *Nazi Empire*, Cambridge, Cambridge University Press, 2010.

imposed transfers.[14] In this perspective, a quick characterization of each of them will have to be the starting point for any analysis of their models of decision-making, coercive diffusion, and their strategy for promoting military occupation regimes.

2 Italian Fascism in the Balkans: Exporting Fascist Institutions

Italian Fascism illustrates the takeover of power by a "united political elite" whose base was a fascist party that was transformed into the primary motor for the institutionalization of the dictatorship. Mussolini did, at times, use the party to retract his concessions to legal/bureaucratic legitimacy, although he lacked the courage and the opportunity to eliminate the "duarchy" that he had inherited: he never abolished the monarchy. Mussolini's attempts to enhance his personal and charismatic authority through the party, state, and cultural apparatus culminated in the creation of the "cult of Il Duce" and in the concentration of decision-making power in the dictator.[15]

The institutionalization of corporatism in Italy is particularly interesting. While it may have been the dominant model in the spread of fascist corporatism, its implementation was one of the slowest and was one with more inter-institutional tensions than other transitions to authoritarianism.[16] Even as an integral part of the Partito Nazionale Fascista (PNF; National Fascist Party) program, quickly outlined in the declaration of principles in its 1927 Charter, it was to take another eleven years for the new system to be integrated and completed through the creation of the Camara dei Fasci e delle Corporazione (Chamber of Fasces and Corporations). Although the Italian Fascist model of corporatism had spread around the world before its institutionalization, the Italian example was characterized by a bicameral political system: an advisory corporatist chamber and a politically controlled senate (with a strong single party and an omnipresent Grand Council).

By the eve of World War II, Italian Fascism had clearly evolved from one phase, which many historians describe as "authoritarian," to

---

[14] Citing Kneuer and Demmelhuber, "We comprehend diffusion to be all transfer of ideas, institutions, and policies characterized as voluntary transfer in contrast to obliged or imposed transfers." Kneuer and Demmelhuber, "Conceptualizing authoritarian gravity centers," p. 46.

[15] See G. Adinolfi, "Political elite and decision-making in Mussolini's Italy," in A. C. Pinto, ed., *Ruling Elites and Decision-Making in Fascist-Era Dictatorships*, New York, Columbia University Press, 2009, pp. 19–54.

[16] See Alessio Gagliardi, *Fascist Italy in the Age of Corporatism. Searching for a Third Way*, London, Routledge, 2024.

one that was more "totalitarian." This was evident in the alliance with Nazi Germany, the introduction of antisemitic legislation (1938), the attempts to permeate Italian society with fascist values, and the regime's expansionist imperialism in Africa, invading Ethiopia in 1935.[17] The decision to enter the war on the side of Germany was made against the opinion of the most conservative sections of the Catholic Church and the army; it was pursued partly through an imperialist project to secure Italy as the hegemonic power in the Mediterranean and the southern Balkans.

In the second half of the 1930s, Mussolini's dictatorship became the most important pole of institutional and ideological diffusion of the Era of Fascism, with its model of personalized leadership, unified political decision-making, and single party and corporatist "organic" representation.

Between its entry into the war and the fall of Mussolini in 1943, Fascist Italy conquered and shared with Nazi Germany several territories in the eastern Mediterranean and the Balkans. Germany and Italy agreed that Albania, Croatia, Montenegro, Greece, and some parts of southern France would be under Italian rule, but tensions emerged among the two occupying powers.[18] In the case of Greece, for example, Germany and Bulgaria had to come to save Italy in 1941. Overall, with their different legal statuses, levels of institution building, and cooperation with local elites, the Italian political dimensions of military occupation were "less fragmented in decision-making compared with Germany, even if knowing some polyocracy as well."[19]

The "Kingdom of Albania"

The case of Albania under Italian occupation represents the only case of occupation in Axis Europe in which Italian Fascism created a political regime that somehow stood for the "ideal type" of exportable Fascist institutions. In 1939, Fascist Italy occupied Albania with a goal of integrating it into an "imperial community."[20] The occupation, as Enriketa

---

[17] See Emilio Gentile, *Storia del Fascismo*, Bari, Laterza, 2022.
[18] On Croatia, see Srdjan Trifković, "Rivalry between Germany and Italy in Croatia, 1942–1943," *Historical Journal*, 36, no. 4 (1993), pp. 879–904. On Italian occupied territories in southern France, see Diane Grillère, *L'Autre Occupation. L'Italie fasciste en France*, Paris, Nouveau Monde Édition, 2023.
[19] P. Fonzi, *Oltre i Confini: Le Occupazione Italiane Durante la Seconda Guerra Mondiale (1939–43)*, Florence, Le Monier, 2020, p. 209. All translations are the author's own.
[20] See Alberto Basciani, *L'impero nei Balcani. L'occupazione italiana dell'Albania 1939–1943*, Roma, Viela, 2022. See also Alexander Lang "Fascist transnationalism during the occupation of Albania (1939–43)," *Modern Italy*, 29, no. 4 (November 2024), pp. 426–440.

Pandelejmoni wrote, "was the culmination of the longer insistence on political and economic domination of Italy upon Albania."[21]

In April 1939, a National Constituent Assembly was called to proclaim the creation of a union between Italy and Albania and to offer the crown of Albania to the King of Italy. The new constitution, the "Basic Statute" of the Kingdom of Albania, was written by Italian jurists to replace the 1928 constitution. As a US law professor wrote in 1939: "The new order in Albania is a model for countries conquered by European dictatorships. The constitutional laws of the kingdom reveal, furthermore, how a modern dictatorship can completely and effectively dominate a vassal state by means of a streamlined organization."[22] According to the statute, the king was the "supreme head of the state" (Article 13) and exercised executive power (Article 6) through a lieutenant general. He concentrated legislative power "with the collaboration of the Consiglio Superiore Fascista Corporativo (Superior Fascist Corporatist Council)" (Article 5), an advisory body consisting of sixty to seventy members of parliament (MPs) that replaced the old parliament. It included the members of the Central Council of the Albanian Fascist Party and effective members of the Consiglio Centrale dell'Economia Corporativa (Central Corporatist Economy Council). Its agenda was defined by its president, no votes were taken in the superior council, and no subject could be placed on the agenda without the king's consent (that is to say, without the consent of the lieutenant general).[23] The Central Corporatist Economy Council was established in 1940 as an advisory body that would prepare *parere* (reports) on all matters relating to economy and labor. It consisted of a president, four vice presidents, and twenty-four members of the Fascist Party. It was organized into four sections: agriculture, industry, commerce, and professions and arts.

The lieutenant general answered politically to the Italian foreign minister. However, he had total administrative control over all political life in Albania. Even if composed of an Albanian prime minister and a council of ministers, the government was controlled by the Italian authorities, and as in many other occupation regimes, each ministry had a permanent Italian counselor attached to it.[24]

---

[21] Enriketa Pandelejmoni, "Under Italian fascist rule. Occupation and collaboration in Albania, 1939–1943," in Pinto and Adinolfi, eds., *Building Dictatorships under Axis Rule*, p. 188.

[22] R. M. W. Kempner, "The new constitution of Albania: A model constitution for European vassal states," *Tulane Law Review*, XV (1940–41), p. 430.

[23] "Fundamental statute of the Kingdom of Albania, June 4, 1939," 143 *British and Foreign State Papers*, N. 327 (1939), pp. 329–330.

[24] E. Papa-Pandelejmoni, "Albania during WWII: Mustafa Merlika Kruja's fascist collaboration," *The European Legacy*, 19, no. 4 (2014), pp. 433–441.

The Albanian Fascist Party (AFP), created as a single party one day before the constitution was approved, was entirely dependent on its Italian counterpart. Defined as "non-native and non-autonomous," but rather as an affiliate of the Italian Fascist Party and as a "voluntary civilian militia" serving Mussolini, the "creator and Duce of Fascism," the AFP intended to create and control other ancillary organizations.[25] In April 1939, Achille Starace, secretary of the Italian Fascist Party, arrived in Albania to announce the foundation of the AFP. The party's central council was one of the two elements in the corporatist chamber that replaced the old parliament. The party exercised considerable influence within local administrations. It controlled several ancillary organizations. The single party also played a leading role in the corporatist organization within the Corporatist Fascist Supreme Council and the Central Corporatist Economy Council.

As Davide Rodogno notes, "The Albanian solution would also probably have been applied to other Balkan countries had not the circumstances of their occupation induced the Fascist regime to take contingent measures that were at variance with the model."[26] In fact, in both Dalmatia and the parts of Slovenia annexed by Italy a panoply of fascist structures was created, including (almost immediately) the corporatist ones.

In Dalmatia, the new governor, *squadrista* Giuseppe Bastianini, set up the Ufficio del Lavoro per la Dalmazia (Dalmatia Labour Office), controlled by the Italian Fascist Party and paving the way for corporatist reform. After the dissolution of the unions and chambers of commerce and industry, Consigli Provinciali delle Corporazioni (Provincial Councils of Corporations) were created.[27] In Slovenia, the attempt to introduce corporatist institutions was clear as well. Mussolini nominated in 1941 a high commissioner for the new "Provincia di Lubiana" and established an advisory "Slovenian Council" charged with the task of assisting the high commissioner. It was formed by fourteen members, including the rector of the University of Ljubljana and representatives of employers and employees of the most important sectors of the economy, "in line with the principles of fascist corporatism."[28] With the creation of the Provincial Workers Union (which was to represent all the unions

---

[25] Cited in S. Trani, ed., *L'Unione fra L'Albania e L'Italia: Censimento Delle Fonti (1939–45) Conservate Negli Archivi Pubblici e Privati di Roma*, Rome, Ministero per I Beni e le Attività Culturali, 2007, p. 45.
[26] Rodogno, *Fascism's European Empire*, p. 60.
[27] Rodogno, *Fascism's European Empire*, p. 124.
[28] T. Ferenc, *La Provincia "Italiana" di Lubiana: Documenti 1941–1942*, Udine, Istituto friulano per la storia del Movimento di liberazione, 1994, p. 48.

of the "Provincia" of Lubiana) and of Consigli Corporativi Provinciali, the institutionalization of corporatism took a step forward, although the plans for the creation of a single party did not materialize.[29] In Slovenia, conservative political Catholicism paved the way for collaboration with Italian Fascism, fostered mainly by Bishop of Lubiana Gregorij Rožman. The dominant political force – the Slovenska Ljudska Stranka (People's Party of Slovenia), headed by Antun Korošec – was a Catholic party subscribing to the corporatist views of the Austrian Christian Social Party, and thus, as one scholar remarked, "ended up by sympathizing with the fascist version of the same ideology."[30] The Italian occupying forces also tried to spread Fascism's mass organizations into the new province of Lubiana with reasonable success until 1943. Plans for the creation of a Montenegrin protectorate along Albanian lines were designed as well.

With the fall of Mussolini in 1943, Germany quickly invaded and occupied Albania and, on Hitler's direct orders, took a very pragmatic attitude toward the local elites. His envoy, Hermann Neubacher, an Austrian Nazi who was already special envoy for economic affairs in Southeastern Europe, recognized Albania's independence and did not constitute a military administration, but only appointed a "German General for Albania."[31] Germany then accepted a collaborationist Regency Council and a Constituent National Assembly that nominated an Albanian government, dissolving all institutional ties to Italy and proclaiming an alliance with the Axis, although formally a "neutral" country.[32]

The "Independent State of Croatia"

After the Axis forces attacked the Kingdom of Yugoslavia on April 6, 1941 and its territory was partitioned between Germany, Italy, Hungary, and Bulgaria, there were some different strategies for political control as well.[33]

---

[29] Gregor Joseph Kranjc, *To Walk with the Devil. Slovene Collaboration and Axis Occupation*, Toronto, The University of Toronto Press, 2013, p. 87.

[30] Marina Cattaruzza, *L'Italia e il confine orientale, 1866–2006*, Bologna, Il Mulino, 2007, p. 161.

[31] On Neubacher, see Stephen G. Gross, *Export Empire German Soft Power in Southeastern Europe, 1890–1945*, New York, Cambridge University Press, pp. 294–310.

[32] Bernd J. Fischer, *Albania at War*, West Lafayette, Purdue University Press, 1999, pp. 171–172. See a very interesting report on German-occupied Albania already written in Berlin by a Wehrmacht officer a few months before the end of the war in Bernd J. Fischer, *Albania, 1943–1945*, Tirana, Albanian Institute for International Studies, 2012, pp. 211–277.

[33] See J. Tomasevich, *War and Revolution in Yugoslavia: Occupation and Collaboration*, Stanford, CA, Stanford University Press, 2001; M.-J. Calic, *History of Yugoslavia*, West Lafayette, ID, Purdue University Press, 2019, pp. 125–141; N. Bartulin, "The NDH as a "Central European bulwark against Italian imperialism": An assessment of

In the case of Croatia, the Axis established the Independent State of Croatia (Nezavisna Država Hrvatska; NDH), with Hitler offering its formal control to fascist Italy. At the same time, most of Serbia was placed under a German administration that gave some powers to a more fragile local government.

The NDH was set up under the political leadership of Ante Pavelić and his Ustasha Croatian Revolutionary Movement (Ustaša – Hrvatski revolucionarni pokret). The Ustasha was a radical ultra-nationalist organization associated with fascism and terrorist political action. Ante Pavelić, a lawyer and extreme-right politician whose main political activity in inter-war Yugoslavia was always associated with the independence of Croatia, went into exile in Germany and Italy on many occasions, which was where he founded the Ustasha.[34] During the 1930s, the movement was increasingly influenced by Italian Fascism and German National Socialism. By the late 1930s, however, it was developing a racist ideology through its demand for a "Gothic" identity for all Croats and by idealizing the peasantry. The Ustasha was fiercely Catholic, identifying Catholicism with Croatian nationalism. As corporatism became an element of ideological convergence between the Croat Catholic movement and Ustasha, most Catholic intellectuals in Croatia supported constructing a social system based on an organic view of society. As the decade progressed, the Ustasha "adapted the Italian Fascist model to Croatian conditions. In the case of corporatism, as on the national question, there was an unmistakable convergence of views between the Ustasha and radical Catholics."[35] The appropriation of German and Italian social policies in the NDH was also very much present, if sometimes in tension.[36]

The NHD "was one of the longest-lasting fascist collaborationist regimes with substantial autonomy and the possibility to develop its own system," and "Ustasha leadership was practically given free hands, of course, for as long as their policies and actions were in line with and did not interfere with those of Nazi Germany or Fascist Italy."[37] In the so-called Roma Treaties of 1941, Pavelić agreed to Italy's control of the

---

Croatian-Italian relations within the German 'new order' in Europe, 1941–45," *Review of Croatian History*, 1 (2007), pp. 49–73.

[34] See G. Miljan, "From obscure beginnings to state 'resurrection': Ideas and practices of the Ustaša organization," *Fascism*, 5 (2016), pp. 3–25.

[35] M. Biondich, "Radical Catholicism and fascism in Croatia, 1918–45," *Totalitarian Movements and Political Religions*, 8, no. 2 (2007), p. 396.

[36] A. Korb, "From the Balkans to Germany and back: The Croatian Labour Service, 1941–45," in Kott and Patel, eds., *Nazism across Borders*, pp. 83–97.

[37] Goran Miljan, "The Ustasha regime, state, and nation-building process state 'independence' in the axis 'New Order'," in Pinto and Adinolfi, eds., *Building Dictatorships under Axis Rule*, p. 124.

NDH Adriatic littoral. Italy formally forced Pavelić to allow the NDH to become a kingdom with an Italian duke – Aimone di Savoia-Aosta, Duke of Spoleto, from the House of Savoia – as King of Croatia, but this was never implemented.

According to one of its main legal theorists, the NDH's principal ideology was nationalism, solidarity, the social obligation of work, and "estate corporatism."[38] Despite its Catholic matrix and the influence of Italian Fascism, as in Slovakia, the corporatist discourse of the leaders and institutions of the NDH was more radical and "socialist." Ethnic cleansing was at the forefront of NDH ideology and one of the basic goals of Ustasha ideology was to create an "ethnically pure Croatia."

The NDH introduced authoritarian and fascist-inspired institutions, even though these were often poorly developed: the single party, a youth organization, a system of national labor, unions, and an outline of "professional organization chambers" as the beginning of a social corporatist system. In 1941, the Ustasha regime established the General League of Estate and Other Fasces (Glavni savez staliških i drugih postrojbi). Although set up within the framework of the Ustasha movement, membership of one of the sixteen – later eighteen – fasces soon became compulsory, as the system's aim was to include and steer all of Croatia's economy and society.

The Ustasha reconvened the Croatian parliament, the Sabor, with reference to the medieval kingdom. Members of parliament were selected by the Ustasha government from among five categories and meetings were convened just a few times after the first session. Its composition resembles the Vichy Conseil National: surviving members of the last Sabor; deputies elected to the Belgrade Legislature on December 8, 1938 and lifetime members of the party's central committee; surviving members of the Council of the Croatian Party of the Right; ranking members of the Ustasha supreme command; and two representatives of the German minority.[39] The State Sabor had nine commissions (treasury, national economy and transportation, education, judiciary and religion, health, cooperatives and corporatism, appeals and petitions, membership, and a house committee). As in almost all authoritarian legislatures, plenary sessions were not to occur except in rare circumstances. The deputies had to ask permission to address the assembly and were prohibited from reading their speeches. Pavelić's signature was

---

[38] Cited in N. Bartulin, *The Racial Idea in the Independent State of Croatia: Origins and Theory*, Leiden, Brill, 2013, p. 146.

[39] Y. Jelinek, "An authoritarian parliament: The Croatian State Sabor of 1942," *Canadian Slavonic Papers / Revue Canadienne des Slavistes*, 22, no. 2 (1980), p. 263.

necessary to validate any law. In 1942, a consultative assembly, the State Council, was created in preparation for a fully corporatist parliament.[40] German reports noted that Pavelić intended to construct a new Sabor with representatives of corporations, and in fact, he often mentioned the idea of a corporatist assembly that was inspired by the Italian corporatist chamber. As in other regimes under Axis rule, different ideas of corporatism had their own areas of influence. The "opposing views about the nature and the future of corporatism in the NDH mirrored the factional infighting in existing corporatist institutions," and the building of several centers of power inside corporatist institutions, mirroring the global tendency of the regime, did not help its consolidation.[41]

The NDH was marked by improvisation, disarticulation between the party and the state, and generalized terrorist violence against all "foreigners," particularly Serbs, Jews, and Roma.

Occupied Greece: A Collaborationist Government without a Political Regime

The military occupation of Greece by German troops was a last-minute supportive answer to the failure of Fascist Italy's invasion of Greece, ironically provoked by Mussolini's fears of the Nazi expansion in the Balkans. Hitler came in support of his Axis partner and invaded Greece from Bulgaria in April 1941. As Mark Mazower wrote, "the Germans had no long-term plans for the country, and Hitler had already decided that a domestic puppet regime would be the least expensive drain on German energies and resources as the invasion of the Soviet Union came closer."[42] Against the wishes of the Greek collaborationist government headed by General Georgious Tsolakoglou, Hitler decided to allow Fascist Italy to participate in the occupation, with Greek administration answering to the two Axis plenipotentiaries, Gunther Altenburg and Pellegrino Ghigi. These two plenipotentionaries, "who had the power to recommend the appointment and dismissal of Greek officials, were the key civilian figures in shaping Axis policy toward Greece."[43]

---

[40] R. Lemkin, *Axis Rule in Occupied Europe, Laws of Occupation, Analysis of Government, Proposals for Redress*, Washington, DC, Carnegie Endowment for International Peace, 1944, pp. 608–609.
[41] L. Marić, "The three fasces of Croatian corporatism, 1941–45," in Pinto, ed., *An Authoritarian Third Way in the Era of Fascism*, p. 161.
[42] Mark Mazower, *Inside Hitler's Greece: The Experience of Occupation, 1941–44*, New Haven, CT, Yale University Press, 1993, p. 18.
[43] Mazower, *Inside Hitler's Greece*, p. 22.

Although always suspicious of fascist Italy, the invaded Greece had had an authoritarian regime since the 1930s. The "Fourth of August" regime in Greece was established in the wake of a coup d'état led in 1936 by the prime minister, Ioannis Metaxas, who was head of a small conservative, anti-parliamentary, and royalist party. Metaxas did not create a single party following the dissolution of parliament and the political parties, as this would have been difficult for the king to accept; however, he did place great hope in the creation of an official youth organization, the National Youth Organization (Ethnikí Orgánosis Neoléas; EON), which was inspired by the fascist model.[44] Metaxas died some months before the German invasion, but although not far in ideological terms from the previous dictatorship, as Aristotle Kallis wrote, "In the end, it is hard to argue that together the three cabinets amounted to a single occupation *regime*; instead, they represented three very different attempts to posit state continuity against a rapidly shifting international and domestic backdrop that they had otherwise very limited control over."[45]

3 Nazi Germany: A "Patchwork" of Dictatorships and Quasi-governments Blinking at Regimes

Hitler's dictatorship was in every aspect of its existence closer to a charismatic regime than any other, and this had significant implications for the operation of the Nazi political system. Hitler's style of rule caused a weakening of the authoritarian state's decision-making structure, resulting in Hitler's rise to absolute power at the head of a system in which the "coexistence [of] and conflict [between] uncoordinated authorities very often undermin[ed] solidarity and uniformity in the exercise of power."[46] Whether as part of a deliberate strategy or merely as a consequence of Hitler's leadership personality, this also provoked a multiplication of ad hoc decisions and ensured that there would be no real or formal limits to his authority.[47] Despite this concentration of power, Hitler's style of rule led him to immerse himself in such matters as the military and the strategic defense and expansion of the Third Reich and to underestimate

---

[44] See Aristotle Kallis, "Ideas in flux ...: the '4th of August' dictatorship in Greece as a political 'departure' in search of 'destination'," in Pinto, ed., *Corporatism and Fascism*, pp. 272–290.

[45] Aristotle Kallis, "State (dis)continuity in occupied Greece. Regimes of emergency," in Pinto and Adinolfi, eds., *Building Dictatorships under Axis Rule*, p. 246.

[46] M. Broszat, *The Hitler State: The Foundation and Development of the Internal Structure of the Third Reich*, London, Longman, 1981, p. 351.

[47] Hans Mommsen, *From Weimar to Auschwitz*, Princeton, NJ, Princeton University Press, 1991, pp. 163–188.

the "command and control" dimension of the administration and of day-to-day domestic politics.

From the perspective of types of military occupation and political administration, one of the most fruitful interpretations of the Nazi political system is that which defines it as a "polyocracy" – a political system that consisted of several decision-making centers, all of which were mediated individually by Hitler.[48] Such a system has many tensions – for example, between the party, its bureaucratic apparatus, and the local and central administrations. However, we should not exaggerate them, since in many cases they complemented each other, "helping the regime to realize its goals."[49]

This polyocratic nature of the Nazi political system would be decisive in the administration of the territories occupied by National Socialist Germany. Here, the option of the "Reichcommissariat" model would be dominant in areas where formally independent states were not authorized. The establishment of a military administration, despite Hitler's initial promises, was rare. It was used almost to the end in Belgium, and especially in the Balkans (Table 1). A Reichcommissar from the Nazi political elite, generally with great political experience and appointed directly by Hitler, directed a complex structure of civilian administration of one or more occupied territories, in coordination with the military occupation structure and having under it a native collaborationist administration. Suffering parallel interference from other political institutions (such as the Party or the SS) either from above or from the side, and some of these also with direct access to Hitler, tensions, as we will see, would always be evident.

The Protectorate of Bohemia and Moravia: A Government without a Regime?

When the German army entered Czechoslovakia in March 1939 and the "Protectorate of Bohemia and Moravia" was proclaimed the following day, the country was already undergoing a process of transition to authoritarianism and of "collaboration" with Nazi Germany. In 1938, having already introduced censorship, parliament passed a special "Enabling Act," which entitled the government to alter the constitution, amend constitutional laws and, in case of "emergency," to rule by decree.[50] President Emile Hácha and Prime Minister Rudolf Beran, a

---

[48] Ernst Fraenkel, *The Dual State*, New York, Oxford University Press, 1942.
[49] Kott and Patel, "Introduction," in Kott and Patel, eds., *Nazism across Borders*, p. 5.
[50] Mary Heimann, *Czechoslovakia. The State That Failed*, New Haven, CT, Yale University Press, 2009, p. 97.

conservative politician and former leader of the Agrarian Party, created the Party of National Unity (PNU; Strana národní Jednoty). It was based on the right-wing and center-right-wing parties, including the small fascist party of Radola Gajda, the National Fascist Community (Národní obec fašistická; NOF). Created in 1938, the PNU was a typical dominant party, "with solid aspirations to transform the country into a new state political project after twenty years of a liberal democratic republic."[51] With a "nationalist, authoritarian, and corporatist ideology," this government-led dominant party was associated with an ongoing plan to establish an authoritarian "corporatist state in the Second Czechoslovak Republic," before the German occupation.[52] "Calibrated collaboration," as Radka Sustrova wrote, was already in the making when Germany established the protectorate.[53]

The first "Reich Protector" was Konstantin von Neurath, former foreign minister of Nazi Germany (1932–1938), but both President Hácha and Prime Minister Rudolf Beran were maintained as heads of the new "protected" state. Contrary to the fears of the conservative collaborationist elite, the German authorities did not offer the fascists any preeminent role in the protectorate. One of the first steps of the government of the establishment of a new political system, with the authorization of the "Reich Protector," and the creation of a single party, largely based on the by-then dissolved PNU: the "National Partnership" (NP). Characterized by a "Christian-oriented traditionalism" associated with a conservative vision of Czech national identity, the first draft of its program designed a corporatist project for the protectorate: "'National life' was to be organized according to three fundamental pillars: national unity, social justice in the corporatist state, and morality and education in the national and Christian spirit."[54]

The most important step in the implementation of social corporatism was the decree issued on June 23, 1939 empowering the Minister of Industry, Commerce, and Handicraft to establish compulsory organizations for

---

[51] Radka Šustrová, "Hácha's Protectorate. Limping corporatism and calibrated collaboration in Bohemia and Moravia under Nazi rule," in Pinto and Adinolfi, eds., *Building Dictatorships under Axis Rule*, p. 50.

[52] Jakub Drábik, "Corporatist models in the ideology of the Czechoslovak national fascist community," in Antonio Costa Pinto, ed., *A Third Authoritarian Way in the Era of Fascism*, London, Routledge, 2022, p. 149.

[53] Šustrová, "Hácha's Protectorate," in Pinto and Adinolfi, eds., *Building Dictatorships under Axis Rule*, p. 40, and R. Šustrová, *Nations Apart: Czech Nationalism and Authoritarian Welfare under Nazi Rule*, Oxford, Oxford University Press, 2024.

[54] Šustrová, "Hácha's Protectorate," in Pinto and Adinolfi, eds., *Building Dictatorships under Axis Rule*, p. 24.

industry, commerce, and crafts, and the creation of the National Trade Union Employees' Headquarters (Národní odborová ústředna zaměstnanecká; NOÚZ), based on the forced unification of hundreds of unions and promising "to unite employees and employers under a single umbrella."[55] Although corporatism was mentioned in internal documents, the word was not used in public. As in Slovakia and other parts of Nazi-occupied Europe, the second "Reich Protector," the SS Obergruppenführer Reinhard Heydrich, who replaced Von Neurath (considered too moderate by Hitler), designed plans for a more Nazi-oriented model in 1942. Suspecting the corporatist projects of the National Partnership, Heydrich made plans to replace it with another organization (headed by the Reich Protector) to prevent "the development of Spann's ideas of a purely 'apolitical' Christian corporatist state."[56] Although not developing these plans, because Hácha was the head of the NP its structure would be transformed in a sort of "cultural and social corporation" in 1942.[57] Social corporatist organizations would change as well to a more Nazi-oriented model.

The Slovak State: "One God, One People, One Party"

The "Slovak State" was created as a result of the breakup of Czechoslovakia in the spring of 1939. It was clearly more autonomous from Nazi Germany than the Protectorate of Bohemia and Moravia. Formally an independent state with de facto and de jure international recognition beyond the Axis, the "Protective Treaty" with Germany in 1939 imposed a number of restrictions on it in the foreign, economic, and military spheres. Part of its border area was controlled by the German army, the Slovak army took part in the war as well, and the Slovak State joined the Axis in 1940.

In the case of the Slovak State, authoritarian political Catholicism, nationalism, and the creation of the National State initially established a political regime that strongly identified with Dollfuss's Austria and the Iberian dictatorships, which then experienced the political intervention of Nazi Germany, limiting and partially altering its political and social institution-building project. As in other countries in Axis Europe,

---

[55] Apparently following the German "Law for the Preparation of the, Organic Reconstruction of German Economy" of 1934. See Moses Moskowitz, "Three Years of the Protectorate of Bohemia and Moravia," *Political Science Quarterly*, 57, no. 3 (1942), p. 365. See also Šustrová, "Hácha's protectorate," in Pinto and Adinolfi, eds., *Building Dictatorships under Axis Rule*, p. 55.

[56] Cited in Šustrová, "Hácha's protectorate," in Pinto and Adinolfi, eds., *Building Dictatorships under Axis Rule*, p. 25

[57] Šustrová, "Hácha's protectorate," in Pinto and Adinolfi, eds., *Building Dictatorships under Axis Rule*, p. 52.

other Nazi institutions, government offices, the Nazi Party, Deutsche Arbeitsfront (DAF; German Labour Front), and the SS were also to be influential in specific areas.

When the Slovak State was created in 1939, Andrej Hlinka's Slovak People's Party (Hlinkova slovenská l'udová strana; HSLS) became the base of single party led by Hlinka's successor and vice chairman, the Catholic priest Józef Tiso, under the motto "One God, One People, One Party."[58] Heavily influenced by Austrian Social Catholics and by Ignaz Seipel, "as early as 1931, [Tiso] moved away from parliamentary democracy by endorsing the Catholic corporatism of *Quadragesimo Anno*."[59] However, despite being the guide of the dictatorship and the single party, Tiso had to share power with Vojtech Tuka, who was more radical, had been appointed prime minister, and whom Nazi Germany wished to retain.[60] In fact, in the single party, the government, and some political institutions, factionalism was clear, with the political elite divided into one group (associated with Tiso) and another more radical faction (led by Tuka).

The new constitution, inspired by Salazar's Portugal and Dolfuss's Austria, sought to reconcile liberal parliamentarianism with corporatism. Within the single party – the Party of National Unity (Strana Slovenskej Národnej Jednoty; SSNJ) – the pro-corporatist clerical faction was initially the most important.[61] The regime's brief existence, Tuka's more radical faction, and the influence of Nazi Germany and the German minority prevented the appearance of a more consolidated corporatist system.[62]

The 1939 constitution proclaimed Slovakia a Catholic state in which "the nation participates in state power through the HSLS," and the single party took control of parliament.[63] The newly created Council of State developed into a corporatist upper house to advise Tiso, who had, in the meanwhile, become president. Members of this privy council included

---

[58] J. K. Hoensch, *Catholics, The State and the European Radical Right, 1919–45*, New York, EEM-Columbia University Press, 1987, p. 174.

[59] J. M. Ward, *Priest, Politician, Collaborator: Jozef Tiso and the Making of Fascist Slovakia*, Ithaca, NY, and London, Cornell University Press, 2013, p. 119.

[60] N. Nedelsky, "The wartime Slovak state: A case study on the relationship between ethnic nationalism and authoritarian patterns of governance," *Nations and Nationalism*, 7, no. 2 (2001), p. 221.

[61] Lemkin, *Axis Rule in Occupied Europe: Laws of Occupation*, p. 142; Y. Jelinek, *The Parish Republic: Hlinka's Slovak People's Party*, New York, EEM-Columbia University Press, 1976, pp. 47–51.

[62] L. Hallon and M. Schvarc, "Ideas, reality and the international context of the social state in the Slovak Republic of 1939–45," *Historický časopis*, 63, no. 5 (2015), pp. 901–937.

[63] Slovak Constitution, July 31, 1939, p. 1. See "Tvorba ústavy Slovenské republiky z 21. července 1939 a cesta k jejímu přijetí," *Právne Historické Studie*, 52, no. 1 (2022), pp. 113–131.

the prime minister, the president of the Slovak assembly, and members nominated by Tiso, the single party, and each corporation (*stände*). Moreover, like Mussolini's Fascist Grand Council, this council, according to chapter five of the constitution, was to choose the candidates for parliament.[64] In a series of articles on the main corporatist principles of the 1939 constitution, a leader of the party and deputy speaker of the Slovak parliament, Karol Mederly, was clear: This "must be built on two basic pillars: the Christian worldview and nationalism. In this way, we will achieve a firm ground of Christian and national solidarity as a basic condition for the Slovak state."[65] As in other dictatorships, the institutionalization of social corporatism was resisted by industrialists, but the most important negative reaction came from the German minority and soon after, from the embassy and the institutions of National Socialism through external intervention, accompanied by Tuka's radical faction, who saw it as the work of a group of "parish priests."[66] In a report to Berlin dated April 1940, the German ambassador stressed the fact that the "Slovak state as a close ally of Nazi Germany could not continue to be directed by the ideology of political Catholicism and it could not be allowed to construct a corporatist system on the ideological basis of the encyclical *Quadragesimo Anno* in the same spirit as the corporatist system of Dollfuss."[67] This lack of trust in the dominant segment of the political elite led Hitler in July 1940 to invite Tiso, Tuka, and Mach (then commander of the Hlinka Guard and chief of the propaganda office) to Salzburg, reinforcing Nazi Germany's position. Germany's interference in Slovakia was further enhanced by the appointment of advisors to key institutions.

In 1942 Tiso received the title of "Leader" from the Slovak assembly in an apparent move to add charismatic elements that could strengthen his position and to present a more global fascistization of the regime. At the same time, Tiso "admitted that neither Catholic corporatism nor a copy of German rule was emerging in Slovakia, but rather 'a combination of both systems'."[68] Tuka and some intellectual politicians close to

---

[64] Hoensch, *Catholics*, p. 180.
[65] Cited in Hallon and Schvarc, "Ideas, reality and the international context of the social state in the Slovak Republic of 1939–45," p. 910.
[66] Hallon and Schvarc, "Ideas, reality and the international context of the social state in the Slovak Republic of 1939–45," p. 915.
[67] Hallon and Schvarc, "Ideas, reality and the international context of the social state in the Slovak Republic of 1939–45," pp. 915–916.
[68] Cited in M. Szabó, "Hitler's priests in Slovakia? On the convergence of Catholicism and fascism in Nazi 'new Europe'," *Czech Journal of Contemporary History*, 29, no. 3 (2022), p. 706.

him developed a corporatist alternative in 1942 that was more compatible with National Socialism through the establishment of a "Slovak working community" organized around "four interest associations, divided according to the type of productive activity and employment, namely the Agricultural Association, Association for Industry, Small Business and Finance, Association of Members of the Free Professions, and the Association of State and Public Employees."[69] The different projects of corporatist reforms were thus a symbol of a dynamic of tension, and among factions in the process of institution-building, of what many defined as a "clerico-fascist" regime in Slovakia.[70]

As in other cases of "German Europe," the authoritarian corporatist regime of Tiso represented the relative autonomy of national elites and a dynamic of tension between political families in respect to the regime's institutional design. But if the corporatist Catholic worldview of the first year was never fully institutionalized, the pro-Nazi radical faction did not dominate either. The final product, as Miloslav Svavo wrote, was "a process of fascist hybridization of Christian nationalism and social Catholicism ... in the context of the power struggle between moderates and radicals, which involved both political and social corporatism."[71]

The "French State": "The House That Pétain Built"

Created following the occupation of France in 1940, the "French State" (called by Clough "the house that Pétain built")[72] although nominally independent and formally retaining its capital in Paris, maintained relative autonomy in a part of France, establishing its seat of government in the city of Vichy. In 1942, however, German and Italian armed forces would occupy the entirety of France. As in other areas of Europe occupied by the Nazi regime, tensions between the occupying authorities emerged. In the words of Marc Olivier Baruch, there were "constant conflicts between the Rue de Lille, headquarters of the embassy headed by Otto Abetz, and the Hotel Majestic on Avenue Kléber, where the services

---

[69] Hallon and Schvarc, "Ideas, reality and the international context of the social state in the Slovak Republic of 1939–45," p. 918.
[70] H. Kubátová and M. Kubát, "The priest and the state: Clerical fascism in Slovakia and theory," *Nations and Nationalism*, 27, no. 3 (2021), pp. 734–749.
[71] Miloslav Szabó, "'Hitler gave the Slovaks a state'. On the fascistization of Christian nationalism and social Catholicism in Tiso's Slovakia, 1939–1942," in Pinto and Adinolfi, eds., *Building Dictatorships under Axis Rule*, p. 66.
[72] S. B. Clough, "The house that Pétain built," *Political Science Quarterly*, 59, no. 1 (1944), pp. 30–39.

of the High Military Commander in France (*Militärsbefehlshaber in Frankreich*, or MBF) were located. Werner Best, one of Heydrich's former collaborators in Gestapo central office in Berlin, was given responsibility for monitoring the French administration. From the spring of 1942, matters relating to repression became autonomous, under the authority of SS General Karl Oberg. The picture was further complicated by the existence of a Franco-German commission, based in Wiesbaden, which had sole responsibility for dealing with relations between the two countries under the armistice agreement."[73]

The first constitutional law of Marshal Pétain's "French State" declares: "The National Assembly concedes all powers to the government of the Republic, under the signature and authority of Marshal Pétain, president of the council, to promulgate one or more acts of the new constitution of the French State. This constitution must guarantee the right to work, families, and the fatherland. It will be ratified by the nation and applied by the assembly to be created."[74]

Pétain and his inner circle presented a public discourse based on an organic view of society, the basis of which were the family, the region, and the profession.[75] Independently of the institutional tensions in the construction of authoritarian political institutions, the dominant cultural model in Vichy, expressed in its propaganda and ideological-legitimation bodies, was "a conscious and organized traditionalism ... that favoured images of a rural, corporatist and religious society."[76]

As Marc-Olivier Baruch wrote, "Pétain's government rallied a strong conservative core, bringing together politicians distanced from power by the Popular Front's success in the 1936 elections, the business bourgeoisie and the Catholic Church hierarchy ... What they all had in common was the primacy given to order, which remained one of the major obsessions of the regime right up to the end, even if the word concealed very different visions." He concluded that "this heterogeneity of sources gave rise to a hybrid regime, closer to Salazar than to Mussolini."[77]

---

[73] Marc Olivier Baruch, "'Not to recognise oneself as a serf is the worst of servitudes'. Marshall Pétain as a dictator, July 1940–August 1944," in Pinto and Adinolfi, eds., *Building Dictatorships under Axis Rule*, p. 92.

[74] Cited in G. Berlia, "La loi constitutionnelle du 10 juillet 1940," *Revue du Droit Public et de la Science Politique*, 60 (1944), pp. 45–57.

[75] M. Cointet-Labrousse, *Vichy et Le Fascisme: Les Hommes, les Structures et les Pouvoirs*, Brussels, Editions Complexe, 1987, p. 179.

[76] P. Ory, "'Preface," in C. Faure, *Le Project Culturel de Vichy*, Lyon, CNRS-Presses Universitaire de Lyon, 1989, p. 7.

[77] Baruch, "Not to recognise oneself as a serf is the worst of servitudes," p. 96.

Corporatism had a strong presence in almost all its varieties in interwar France, from fascists to conservative Catholics and technocrats.[78] In fact, of all the regimes associated with the Nazi occupation, Vichy was the one in which corporatism had by far the greatest presence and, significantly, where it was most rooted ideologically among the political elite, their institutions, and their propaganda. The "Révolution nationale" also marked the colonial universe that survived under its control. Nevertheless, while social corporatism made a real attempt to become institutionalized, the same cannot be said of political corporatism, which was only vaguely sketched out in some constitutional projects. Salazar's Estado Novo (New State), as the majority of students of Vichy corporatism stress, fascinated an important segment of the French radical right, who saw in it a model that avoided the "revolutionary rhetoric of Italian Fascism."[79]

Like other dictators of the time, Pétain used several constitutional acts to concentrate legislative power to his person and ensured that ministers answered to him alone. Both the parliament and senate were suspended before being closed entirely in 1942. Later, in the context of a difficult regime coalition and Nazi demands, Pétain created the office of Vice President of the Council for Pierre Laval and increased the powers of a head of government, giving it a more bicephalous character.

The single party that had often been discussed in Vichy was never institutionalized. Against the background of a tense "limited pluralism," which included Catholics and liberal conservatives as well as fascist parties, internal tensions hindered its effective institutionalization, determining the centrality of a controlled administration.[80] In 1940, Marcel Déat assembled a small group of MPs of varying tendencies and created the "Commission for the Creation of the National Single Party" (Le comité de constitution du parti national unique; CCPNU). Written with a clear purpose of unifying several political tendencies, the draft of its manifesto sent to Pétain included "the organization of economic life in a syndicalist and corporatist

---

[78] See O. Dard, "Vichy France and corporatism," in Pinto, ed., *Corporatism and Fascism*, pp. 216–225.

[79] A. Chatriot, "Un débat politique incertain: Le corporatisme dans la France des années 1930," *Etudes Sociales*, 157–8 (1and 2) (2013), p. 238. See O. Dard and I. Sardinha-Desvignes, "Vichy and the Salazarist model," in Pinto, ed., *An Authoritarian Third Way in the Era of Fascism*, pp. 107–121.

[80] M. O. Baruch, *Servir l'État Français: L'Administration en France de 1940 à 1944*, Paris, Fayard, 1997.

way under the control of the State."[81] However, without Pétain's green light and decisive intervention, Déat could not force the unification of conservatives and the various fascist parties from above. Other projects were developed – however, none were to be institutionalized.

The labor charter – the law on the "social organization of professions" – was introduced in October 1941.[82] Inspired by Fascist Italy, Franco's Spain, and Salazar's Portugal, and with the powerful presence of corporatist economists, law professors, technical experts, and former union leaders, it established compulsory union membership and outlawed strikes, organizing the world of work into twenty-nine professional families. The report addressed to Marshal Pétain introducing the law stressed that the purpose of the charter was clear: "the creation of future corporations that are the great hopes for France's future."[83]

The Conseil National was tasked with drafting a constitution, and its commission presented four different drafts to Marshal Pétain. The first projects opted for authoritarian and corporatist models, mainly inspired by the 1933 Portuguese constitution, to evolve later toward a "rationalized parliamentarism."[84] In one of the first versions, the National Assembly had a non-elected "Grand Council" and a corporatist "National Council." The second one, known as the "Gignoux" project after its author, Claude-Joseph Gignoux, is more organic in its several versions. Its main principles were "*famille, travail, patrie*" (family, work, fatherland), "professional suffrage," and a bicameral National Assembly that was closer to the integralist corporatist type of representation.[85]

At the beginning of 1944, Pétain approved a constitutional project to introduce a compromise between liberal and light corporatist representation; it never came into force. By that time the Germans had demanded the departure of Pétain's closest collaborators and forced the participation in government of more radical fascist actors (like Darnand, and later, Marcel Déat) who were better prepared for a more mobilizing political and ideological "collaboration" with Nazi Germany in the last phase of the war.

---

[81] J.-P. Cointet, "Marcel Déat et le Parti Unique (Été 1940)," *Revue d'histoire de la Deuxième Guerre mondiale*, 91 (1973), p. 7.
[82] See J.-P. le Crom, *Syndicats, Nous Voilà! Vichy et le Corporatisme*, Paris, Editions del'Atelier, 1995.
[83] Cited in L. Baudin, *Le Corporatisme*, Paris, Librairie General de Droit et de Jurisprudence, 1942, p. 213.
[84] See E. Le Floch, "Les projets de constitution de Vichy (1940–44)," doctoral thesis in constitutional law, Université de Paris Pantheon-Assas, 2003.
[85] Cointet, *Le Conseil National de Vichy 1940–44*, pp. 301–306.

Nedić's Serbia: "Labor, Family, and Nation"

In military-occupied Serbia after the brief "Commissars Government" of May to August 1941, the German authorities established a domestic "Government of National Salvation" with very limited powers from September 1941 to October 1944 with the conservative General Milan Nedić at its head.[86] Nedić "envisioned an ultraconservative rather than a fascist Serbian state and stood closer to Pétain than to Ante Pavelić."[87] Ironically, in order to fashion institutions and government policy, Nedić turned to Dimitrije Ljotić, the former justice minister in the royal dictatorship of King Alexander in Yugoslavia, who had resigned after the rejection of his project of corporatist constitution. After his brief time in government, Ljotić became leader of Zbor, a radical-right party based on small fascist groups created in 1935. Initially strongly influenced by the teachings of Action Française, Ljotić blended it with the institutional model of Italian Fascism. Its political program was a mixture of corporatism and anti-liberalism in the political and economic sphere, associated with an anti-Semitic nationalism.[88]

General Nedić, probably emulating Pétain, always cited the motto, "labor, family, and nation" in his speeches.[89] As with the NDH in neighboring Croatia, several social corporatist organizations were established. Dimitrije Ljotić and other supporters of "organic sociology" campaigned once more for the merits of the corporatism state, which would demonstrate the "resurgent, persistent, and flexible nature of corporatist theories in the Serbian context."[90]

The Government of National Salvation "attempted on several occasions to secure a better position for itself and Serbia within the German 'New Europe'."[91] Milan Nedić submitted different memoranda to the military commander of Serbia outlining the plan of the government to transform Serbia into a "Peasant Cooperative State" with him as the "State Leader" – that is, the head of the government and the supreme

---

[86] See the excellent research of Z. Janjetović, *Collaboration and Fascism Under the Nedić Regime*, Belgrade, Institute for Recent History of Serbia, 2018, pp. 441–448.

[87] A. Prusin, *Serbia under the Swastika: A World War II Occupation*, Champaign, University of Illinois Press, 2017, p. 68.

[88] M. Martic, "Dimitrije Ljotic and the Yugoslav national movement Zbor, 1935–45," *East European Quarterly*, 14, no. 2 (1980), pp. 219–239; J. P. Newman, *Yugoslavia in the Shadow of War*, Cambridge, Cambridge University Press, 2015, pp. 228–229.

[89] Newman, *Yugoslavia in the Shadow of War*, p. 67.

[90] See T. Kuljic, "Serbian fascism and sociology," *Sociologija*, 16, no. 2 (1974), pp. 237–268.

[91] See Rastko Lompar, "The Nedic Regime in Occupied Serbia Conflicting Loyalties and Aims,"in Pinto and Adinolfi, eds., *Building Dictatorships under Axis Rule*, pp. 165–186.

commander of the army. The creation of a ruling single party, although supported by some, was not included in the plan.

Included in the plans to improve the status of Serbia presented by Nedić to (and rejected by) the Nazi authorities, the project to build a new "organic" political structure for the creation of a Serbian state also included a representational structure that would be articulated through several "people's chambers" at the village, municipality, and state level. It was conceived as a hierarchical and nonelected structure leading to a "National Assembly of Serbia" (which would be directed by state leadership and would only have advisory powers). All decision-making power would be in the hands of the head of government, General Nedić, as the "first master of the people."[92] This draft plan was sent in two memorandums to the German occupation administration, which rejected the project after some hesitation, with the commanding general in Serbia, Paul Bader, suggesting Italy had been behind the proposal.

Quisling's Norway under Fascism: "National Revolution from Above"

The occupation of Norway in 1940 and the different projects of administration to be established are another clear example of the competing projects of Nazi agencies and Hitler's decisions. In this case, there was hesitation in offering power to Vidkun Quisling, the head of a small fascist party, and the appointment of Josef Terboven as Reichskommissar. Terboven attempted initially "a conservative authoritarian, rather than Nazi, solution to the problem of who would administer the country under German occupation," only to later opt for the second, based on Hitler's decision.[93] As Stein Larsen wrote, "Quisling, as the principal agent, became caught between the competing agendas of the two German agencies. However, both were ultimately subject to Hitler's final decision."[94]

Quisling's brief and limited "national revolution from above" in Nazi-occupied Norway represents the takeover of (limited) power by a small fascist party,[95] National Unity (Nasjonal Samling; NS), which was

---

[92] M. Ristović, "Rural 'anti-utopia' in the ideology of Serbian collaborationists in the Second World War," *European Review of History: Revue européenne d'histoire*, 15, no. 2 (2008), p. 187.

[93] P. Morgan, *Hitler's Collaborators: Choosing between Bad and Worse in Nazi-occupied Western Europe*, Oxford, Oxford University Press, 2018, p. 62.

[94] Stein U. Larsen, "Norway under Vidkun Quisling. 'Not Guilty!',"Pinto and Adinolfi, eds., *Building Dictatorships under Axis Rule*, p. 114.

[95] Quisling cited in H. F. Dahl, *Quisling: A Study in Treachery*, Cambridge, Cambridge University Press, 1999, p. 244.

influenced by National Socialism and Italian Fascism in both its ideology and political program, but was closer to Nazi Germany in its international relations.[96] On the very first day of the Nazi occupation of Norway, Vidkun Quisling, the leader of NS, led an initially unsuccessful coup against the Norwegian government. Sometime later, though, NS became the single party and the main instrument of Norwegian collaboration. During one of these phases, the Nazis gave the Norwegian authorities some scope for maneuvering and the political autonomy with which to construct a regime under occupation. When the opportunity arose at the end of 1942, Reichskommissar Terboven announced the transfer of power to Quisling, who was appointed president minister of an "autonomous government." The Reichskommissariat oversaw the most important decisions, and German supervisors were in place in every major department of government and administration.

When Quisling was appointed to this position, according to one of his biographers, his intentions were threefold: "to conclude peace with Germany; introduce a corporatist state; and summon a council of the Kingdom."[97] Social corporatism under NS rule was given its first push with the creation of the Office for Corporations within the Ministry of the Interior in 1941. Almost all voluntary associations were to be registered and "to become corporate members of the state."[98] This process of institutionalizing a "labor corporation" faced strong and partially unexpected resistance from organized interests, with even civil servants fearing the domination of the state apparatus by the party and expressing their discontent to the German authorities.[99] The same happened with the labor code, blocked by Terboven, although always present in Quisling's speeches.[100]

Quisling's plan was quite clear as it was implemented: the creation of autonomous guilds (corporations) "along Italian lines."[101] The organization of guilds licensed by the state and the new basis for a national assembly to replace the old parliament was the realization of the

---

[96] See Dahl, *Quisling: A Study in Treachery*, pp. 110–117; S. U. Larsen, "Charisma from below? The Quisling case in Norway," in A. C. Pinto, R. Eatwell and S. U. Larsen, eds., *Charisma and Fascism in Interwar Europe*, London, Routledge, 2007, pp. 97–106.

[97] See P. M. Hayes, *Quisling: The Career and Political Ideas of Vidkun Quisling, 1887–1945*, Newton Abbot, David and Charles, 1971, p. 278.

[98] Dahl, *Quisling*, p. 212.

[99] See O. K. Hoidal, *Quisling: A Study in Treason*, Oslo, Norwegian University Press, 1989, pp. 575–578.

[100] See Mats Ingulstad, "Under the hard law of war: Norwegian social reforms under German influence," in Kott and Patel, eds., *Nazism across Borders*, p. 252.

[101] Dahl, *Quisling*, p. 211.

"New Order's" authoritarian representation. Only the state-organized guilds were represented. A memorandum from the Ministry of the Interior detailed the number of representatives sent by each corporatist body, noting that members of the single party "would be required to function as delegates." In total, there were one hundred and twenty representatives from the thirteen corporations, of which six had been established by the spring of 1942.[102] This corporatist advisory parliament, the Riksting, consisted of two chambers: the Næringsting (Economic Chamber) and the Kulturting (Cultural Chamber).

Students of Quisling's short rule in Norway offer different reasons for the abrupt end to the project to convene the Riksting and institutionalize the National Assembly. Among the reasons was that this Riksting, with its limited authority, did not have the unanimous support of the NS leadership, who feared the old parties would infiltrate it. There was also some resistance from organized interests, particularly from within the economic sector, to their forced integration into the state (while the Nazi authorities, fearing social conflict, viewed this forced integration with suspicion). Reichskommissar Terboven found the situation critical and foresaw a situation where vital German interests could be threatened. However, the most plausible explanation may be the social resistance to "corporatization" and the lack of belief that Quisling's controlled assembly could be trusted as state organs. Quisling then decided to make plans for a legislature that was based on the single party rather than on the corporations. However, he decided to make the Næringsting and Kulturting advisory bodies to the Ministries of Industry and Culture, respectively. He announced this plan at the NS convention in September 1942. He informed the party that a new constitution would have to create a new political representation based on the single party. The corporatist chambers should be, in his own words, "exclusively of a professional and not a political nature."[103]

The resistance of interest groups (encouraging resignations and denials) to participate in the new institutions and the fear of social turmoil provoked the intervention of Reichskommissar Terboven; he canceled the Riksting plan, with Quisling receiving a message from Berlin telling him to stop until the war was won. As a result, "Quisling's vision of a corporatist Riksting as the basis for a new form of representative body was left in tatters, and his hopes of signing a peace treaty with Hitler, in which

---

[102] Hayes, *Quisling*, p. 285; Dahl, *Quisling*, p. 274.
[103] Cited in Dahl, *Quisling*, p. 277.

Norway would become an independent state within the German federal union, was ended."[104]

The "Italian Social Republic": Italian Fascism under Nazi Rule

Some military occupation regimes were not the product of calculated imperialist expansion, but simply of the unexpected consequences of the development of the war; the overthrow of Mussolini in July 1943, some days after the invasion of Sicily by the Allies Armies, was another clear case. Ideological and political radicalization, improvisation, and the growing role of the fascists as political actors in Axis Europe are the main characteristics of this last period of the war in Europe.

The "Italian Social Republic" (RSI), led by Benito Mussolini from September 1943 to April 1945 in the German-occupied center-north of Italy after his release from prison by a military operation, is a clear example of the ideological, political, and social radicalization of fascism. The RSI is also sometimes characterized as a "nazification" of Italian Fascism, but in the social and economic dimension, it was Nazi Germany that "moderated" RSI's "social" impetus, mainly using pragmatic war-related factors.[105]

Even before Mussolini was liberated from a fortress in the Abruzzi, Germany was already making plans for a new Italian regime in the areas under German military control. Hitler nominated then-diplomat Rudolf Rahn as German plenipotentiary to the "national Fascist Italian government." For the purpose of this Element, the more interesting analytical dimensions of the RSI refer to institutional reforms and projects of new political and social institutions, looking at "the process of legitimation of the new government toward both the Germans and the Italians" and to the model those fascist elites "claimed to represent, since the new political space and geographical territory were born without a state."[106] With the Italian royal family already in southern Italy (occupied by the Allies' armed forces), Mussolini made his first speech from Munich, announcing the creation of the Republican Fascist Party (PFR) and shortly afterwards of the "Italian Social Republic." The seat of government was eventually

---

[104] Stein U. Larsen, "Corporations against corporatism in Quisling Norway, 1940–1950s," in Pinto and Finchelstein, eds., *Authoritarianism and Corporatism in Europe and Latin America*, p. 104.

[105] For a "polyocratic" approach to the German Occupation of Italy, see Lutz Klinkhammer, *L'occupazione tedesca in Italia: 1943–1945*, Turin, Bollati Boringhieri, 2016.

[106] Adinolfi, "The Italian social republic legitimation struggles and unfulfilled visions," in Pinto and Adinolfi, eds., *Building Dictatorships under Axis Rule*, p. 210.

installed in the town of Saló and several ministries were dispersed in the neighborhoods and throughout northern Italy, always with German control institutions nearby.

The selection of ministers for the new government was decided in Germany by Mussolini and Alessandro Pavolini, a fascist of *prima hora*, under the supervision of Rudolf Rahn. They were almost all veteran fascists, from which five were former ministers (including Pavolini, Minister of Popular Culture). The Verona Congress held in November 1943 approved the political program of the new regime, now with a more anti-plutocratic, social, and corporatist rhetoric, and a more ideological and paramilitary PRF, directed by Alessandro Pavolini. According to the "manifest" approved in the Congress, a new constituent assembly was to be created, composed of members of the fascist trade unions and representatives of the occupied provinces, and the Chamber of Fasces and Corporations (Camera dei fasci e delle corporazioni) would be reorganized. The Labor Charter (Carta del Lavoro) remained the fundamental programmatic act, but it was announced already the new pillar of social corporatism to be created: the Confederazione Generale del Lavoro, della Tecnica e delle Arti (CGLTA), formally founded in December 1943. The manifesto did not forget to consider Italian Jews foreigners and enemies as well, a radicalization of an anti-Semitism already present in the Italian fascist regime since the mid 1930s.

The writing of the new constitution was assigned to the minister Carlo Alberto Biggini, one of the few fascist jurists with a prominent position among the elite of Saló. Presented to the government in December 1943, the approval of the project was postponed until a stabilization of the war scene in Italy. Now a republic, Article 1 of the draft of the constitution described the "organic" nature of "the Italian nation," defined as "a political and economic organism which performs it activities based on its civil, religious, linguistic, juridical, ethical and cultural lineage."[107] The Catholic religion was the only religion of the RSI and there were concessions to elected institutions, although the new constituent assembly was to be composed of members of the fascist trade unions, agriculture, and representatives of the occupied provinces. This assembly would elect the "Duce of the Italian Republic." A "Chamber of the Representatives of Work" and a senate with a corporatist structure was also foreseen in the project.

---

[107] See *Acta della Fondazione della R. S. I.- Instituto Storico*, Gennaio-Marzo, 2020, pp. 3–13.

The most polemic agenda of the RSI was the one of the "socialization of the economy," announced in the Verona Congress and in the project of the Constitution. Angelo Tarchi, Minister of the Corporatist Economy, started the process in 1944 with several decree-laws, through which the management of the firms was to be "comprised of technicians, CGLTA members, and managers in order to make decisions."[108] Nationalizations started in the end of 1944, but, under pression from German authorities, the process was delayed: "Knowing that the Germans greatly benefited from their many war orders to Italian factories, they could count on Nazi protection from Mussolini's neo-Corporatism."[109]

Arrow Cross's "Government of National Unity" in Hungary

The coming to power of the fascists of the Arrow Cross Party, after the invasion of Hungary by Nazi troops in 1944, is the final paradigmatic case of a small fascist party taking on the role of supporter of last resort in German Europe. Although often blocked and limited in their access to power and in their ability to constitute the basis of political regimes of occupation, under Axis Rule in Europe, the fascists were the most faithful allies, always available for the political and repressive radicalization associated with the war.

With a right-wing authoritarian regime since the 1920s, the stabilization of Hungary (following the successful counter-revolution of 1919–20) gave rise to a competitive authoritarian regime under the paternal but firm leadership of Admiral Miklós Horthy. When in October 1932 Horthy reluctantly appointed Gyula Gömbös Prime Minister – despite the fragmentation of the Hungarian extreme right – the regime began to move to the radical right. Gömbös, known as Gombolini by his political enemies, had been the leader of a right-wing paramilitary association and was a close associate of Horthy, who nevertheless mitigated the most radical parts of the former's strategy. An ex-Minister of Defense, Gömbös became Prime Minister and opened a new political style by touring the country announcing this new program. Although vague in many ways, once in power Gömbös and his faction began to show clear signs of opting for a dictatorial model. He reorganized the dominant party, renamed it the Party of National Unity (Nemzeti Egység Pártja; NEP), provided it with a

---

[108] Adinolfi, "The Italian Social Republic Legitimation Struggles and Unfulfilled Visions," p. 223.
[109] H. James Burgwyn, *Mussolini and the Salò Republic, 1943–1945. The Failure of a Puppet Regime*, Cham, Palgrave, 2018, p. 133.

small paramilitary section, and turned its attention to mass mobilization. More importantly, it was given a more hierarchical structuring, controlling social and professional organizations.

Despite the fascist influence on Gömbös's projects, the models of Dollfuss's Austria and Salazar's Portugal were the dominant ones in Hungary.[110] After the death of Gömbös, corporatist projects were present in some of their successors, like Béla Imrédy and Pal Telekit (1939–1941). The latter, while strengthening anti-Semitic legislation and dealing with the outbreak of the war and German rule, continued the institutionalization of social corporatism and presented a draft of a constitutional reform with the corporatist reform of Parliament. As one of his biographers remarks, Teleki, as well as other segments of the conservative Hungarian elites, believed that a "professional Government" restructured according corporatism lines "was more suitable for meeting the demands of the day."[111] As in previous projects, in the draft of the Constitution both the Lower and Upper Houses would have been filled with delegates selected by the counties and representatives of the socio-economic corporations. Political parties would almost disappear, along with the representatives of the aristocracy in the Upper House. The plans of "the priest of the Nation" were not enthusiastically received by the elite, but "the increasingly complex foreign policy matters were not conducive to major legislative innovations."[112]

It was this "competitive authoritarian" regime, progressively influenced by the radical right but with few concessions to the local fascists, that would be integrated into the Nazi "New Order." As Istvan Deak wrote, "Germans followed amazingly moderate policies in Hungary."[113] Benefiting from some territorial expansion and becoming the fourth member to join the Axis powers when it signed the Tripartite Pact, Horthy's regime did not suffer much conditioning from Germany in the configuration of its political system. At the same time that the internal conjuncture was radicalizing, the fascist Arrow Cross (which achieved some electoral successes in the 1930s, between repressive attacks and returns to legality) was always excluded from power.

---

[110] For a detailed study on the debates and corporatist projects in Hungary, see Miklós Szalai, "Újrendiség és Korporativizmus a Magyar Politikai Gondolkodásban (1931–1944)," *Multunk*, 47, no. 1 (2002), pp. 52–105.
[111] Balázas Ablonczy, *Pál Teleki (1874–1941). The Life of a Controversial Hugarian Politician*, New York, EEM-Columbia University Press, 2006, p. 223.
[112] Ablonczy, *Pál Teleki (1874–1941)*, p. 224.
[113] Istvan Deak, "Collaborationism in Europe, 1940–1945: The Case of Hungary," *Austrian History Yearbook*, 15 (January 1979), p. 154.

It was not until 1944, in the face of Horthy's secret negotiations with the Allies and the corresponding invasion of Hungary by German troops, that Szálasi and the Arrow Cross Party were installed in power, forming a "Government of National Unity" that would last a few months. Their government was short-lived, but they had a clearly prepared model for their political regime. As Catherine Horel wrote, "The party had carefully prepared for coming to power by drafting a constitution and legislative proposals."[114] Szálasi immediately took the name "Leader of the Nation" (*Nemzetvezető*) and tried to implement his plan of regime-building by creating a hierarchical corporatist structure with fourteen corporations. The Dolgozo Nemzet Hivatás Rendje (Corporatist Order of the Working Nation) was then presented and adopted by decree. At the same time, the Arrow Cross Party had put their men in key positions of what remained of the state apparatus, and its militia was on the forefront of anti-Semitic violence until its retreat to Austria with the German army.

Netherlands: A Reichskommissar with Fascist Supporting Party

After the German invasion of the Netherlands in May 1940 and the exile of the Dutch government in the UK, the occupying power installed an occupation structure similar to that of Norway. The German armed forces initially intended to establish a military administration with a predominant position vis-à-vis other Nazi institutions, such as the Party or the SS, but Hitler appointed a Reichskommissar, Arthur Seyss-Inquart, former Governor of Austria after the Anschluss, that stayed "directly" subordinate to him (that is, to the head of the Reich Chancellery). However, as has been pointed out by G. Hirschfeld, "The fundamental polyocracy of the Nazi system, the cooperation and competition between rival groups, institutions, and individuals, and their divergent interests, methods, and intentions – these are nowhere more nakedly revealed than in occupation policy of the Netherlands."[115] In fact, "the tasks and functions of the Generalkommissare were characterized by a permanent dualism."[116] The appointment of representatives of the Nazi Party and of the SS guaranteed that both institutions "would be able to fight for

---

[114] Catherine Horel, "The Short-lived national-socialist arrow- cross government in Hungary: imported fascism vs. local conservatism?," in Pinto and Adinolfi, eds., *Building Doctatoships under Axis Rule*, p. 139.

[115] G. Hirschfeld, *Nazi Rule and Dutch Collaboration: The Netherlands under German Occupation 1940–45*, Oxford, New York and Hamburg, Berg, 1988, p. 44.

[116] Hirsghfeld, *Nazi Rule and Dutch Collaboration*, p. 44.

their own political ideas in the Netherlands, if necessary, against the Reichskommissar himself."[117]

Soon after the occupation, some leading Dutch conservative and radical right leaders proposed the creation of a party with an anti-parliamentary and corporatist program – the Netherlands Union (Nederlandse Unie; NU) – and began negotiations with the German administration. Its proponents came from various conservative anti-parliamentary and corporatist groups.[118] The fascists of Anton Mussert's National Socialist Movement in the Netherlands (Nationaal-Socialistische Beweging; NSB) immediately presented themselves as an alternative of governance as well. The NSB, the most important Dutch fascist party, had suffered the classic ups-and-downs of some European fascist parties in the 1930s. Created in 1931, it reached its electoral peak in the 1935 elections, winning nearly eight percent of the vote, to decline in the following years.[119] Closer in programmatic terms to the NSDAP, Mussert entertained the hope of being appointed head of a fascist occupation regime, after meetings with Hitler. Although he did not unleash a coup d'état like Quisling, he thought that "after eight years of struggle, the day has come to harvest."[120]

The NU, as a collaborationist party, sought to reorganize Dutch society as "conservative nationalist, authoritarian, and corporatist alternative to both the fascism of the NSB and the by then defunct democratic parliamentary system."[121] As one of his students wrote, "At root it clearly owed most to social Catholic and corporatist thought. But in it were also distilled the various elements of traditionalism, nationalism, anti-capitalism, and anti-Marxism which flourished throughout Western Europe in the inter-war period."[122] Intending to create a "loyal relationship" with the occupation authorities, "The program established a tripartite structure with political, cultural, and socio-economic sectors ... and a 'strong Dutch people closely linked with the overseas colonies'; 'under the

---

[117] Hirsghfeld, *Nazi Rule and Dutch Collaboration*, p. 25.
[118] Gerhard Hirschfeld, "Collaboration and attentism in the Netherlands 1940–41," *Journal of Contemporary History* 16 (1981), pp. 467–486.
[119] See Dietrich Orlow, *The Lure of Fascism in Western Europe: German Nazis, Dutch and French Fascists, 1933–1939*, New York, Palgrave, 2009.
[120] Cited in J. M. Damsma, "Nazis in the Netherlands: A social history of national socialist collaborators, 1940–1945," Thesis, fully internal, Universiteit van Amsterdam, 2013, p. 21.
[121] Morgan, *Hitler's Collaborators*, p. 74. For references to the Salazar's corporatism from some of its leaders, see Robin de Bruin, "Portuguese Salazarism as an example for a third way 'renewal' in the Netherlands, 1933–1946," in Pinto, ed., *An Authoritarian Third Way*, pp. 83–84.
[122] M. L. Smith, "Historians and the problem of the Nederlandse Unie," *History*, 72, no. 235 (June 1987), p. 256.

leadership of a vigorous and enterprising authority,' with the population organised itself in an 'organic structure'."[123] By February 1941, the NU already had a total of 800,000 members. The NU even discussed the draft of a constitution that was never publicized. Written by a former leader of the Roman Catholic State Party, it envisaged as a system of representation "a hybrid of parliamentary and corporatist bodies and called for extensive restrictions on Dutch party pluralism."[124] Even though he was a latecomer to the NSDAP and the SS, after participating in the Cabinets of Dollfuss and Schuschnigg in Austria, "it is hard to believe that Seyss-Inquart had much taste for these ideas himself, particularly after his experiences with the Austrian form of a corporatist state."[125] In fact, the NU program referred not only to the introduction of an authoritarian version of social corporatism, but also of political corporatism. Predictably, the NSB denounced the NU as a "product of reactionary political Christianity."[126] But their fascist alternative, "containing an authoritarian, corporatist Dutch state with limited sovereign rights in alliance with a Germanic leadership state," although it was presented repeatedly to Hitler, did not succeed either.[127] Nevertheless, Seyss-Inquart dissolved the NU in December 1941, ending the hopes of a collaborationist regime of the Dutch radical-right, and recognized the NSB as the only legal party in occupied Netherlands. While refusing Mussert's ambitions to govern, the fascists became the sole political partner (with all other parties dissolved), with ambitions to lead the Dutch colonies as well.[128]

While his plays for power (the last of which was in 1942, in a meeting with Hitler) were rejected, apparently on the basis of Quisling's negative experience in Norway, Mussert was allowed to be formally the "Leader of the Dutch Nation" and to have a Political Secretariat giving "advice" to the Reichskommissar and penetrating the local political administration. The occupation model, however, continued to be based on a direct and controlled relationship with the Dutch public administration.

As in Belgium, the secretaries-general of the ministries, reorganized and purged of Jews in particular, formed the basis for administration of the occupied Netherlands, with the Council of Secretaries-General developing

---

[123] Hirschfeld, *Nazi Rule and Dutch Collaboration*, p. 71.
[124] Cit. in Smith, "Historians and the problem of the Nederlandse Unie," p. 255.
[125] Hirschfeld, *Nazi Rule and Dutch Collaboration*, pp. 85–86.
[126] Cited in Hirschfeld, *Nazi Rule and Dutch Collaboration*, p. 86.
[127] Hirschfeld, *Nazi Rule and Dutch Collaboration*, p. 281
[128] Jennifer L. Foray, "An old empire in a new order: The global designs of the Dutch Nazi Party, 1931–1942," *European History Quarterly*, 43, no. 1 (2013), pp. 27–52.

"from a purely internal communications group into a collective body for decision-making and representation."[129] Now stripped of any elective principle, the same happened in regional and local government. In the latter field, the NSB's presence had increased considerably. By 1944, fifty-two percent of the Dutch population lived in municipalities administered by NSB and thirty-four percent of mayors were from Mussert's party.[130]

Another field of collaboration with Mussert's Fascists – moreover, one rigorously established by Reich Commissioner Seyss-Inquart – was to do with the implementation of social corporatism along Nazi lines and based on the model of the equivalent German institutions. "The vocational principle of organization" was introduced "in the liberal professions, health and veterinary care, the administration of justice and culture, as well as in commerce, agriculture and labour organisations," and "the compulsory membership of all members of a profession in the appropriate corporation" was institutionalized, named in some cases "chambers," like the Chamber of Culture, "estates," like the Agricultural Estate, or "fronts," like the Labor Front, and covering almost every profession.[131] In some cases, the Reichskommissariat blended some of these compulsory elements of the corporatist structure with the ones of the NSB, like the Dutch Agricultural Estate, provoking negative reactions.[132]

On the eve of the occupation, the Dutch trade union confederations were organized along party and cultural-religious camps, the most important of which was associated with the Social Democrats, followed by the Catholic and Protestant camps: the Netherlands Association of Trade Unions (Nederlands Verbond van Vakverenigingen), Roman Catholic Workmen's Association (Rooms Katholiek Werkliedenverbond), and the Christian National Trade Union (Christelijk Nationaal Vakverbond). These trade union confederations were supported by a small galaxy of mutual and welfare associations. Seyss-Inquart's strategy was to appoint the head of the trade union department of the NSB, H. Woudenberg, to the post of trade union commissioner and to force the unions to merge into one under his leadership. These steps formed part of his path toward the creation of the Dutch Labor Front in 1942. Initially collaborative,

---

[129] Hirschfeld, *Nazi Rule and Dutch Collaboration*, p. 136.
[130] Werner Warmbrunn, *The Dutch under German Occupation, 1940–45*, Stanford, CA, Stanford University Press, 1963, p. 38.
[131] Hirschfeld, *Nazi Rule and Dutch Collaboration*, p. 38.
[132] Hirschfeld, *Nazi Rule and Dutch Collaboration*, pp. 38–39.

many trade unionists, starting with the Catholics, would later distance themselves, and their unions dissolved.[133]

Although under German control, it was the secretaries-general who created and reorganized the new corporatist economic institutions, namely the Secretary-General of the Department of Economic Affairs, by creating two organizations by decree: the Zelfstandige Organisatie ter Ontwikkeling van het Bedrijfsleven (commonly known as the Woltersom Organization); and the Organisatie voor de Voedselvoorziening (Organization of Food Supply). Both were employers' organizations. Finally, after some negotiations with the most important economic interest groups, the Nationaal Comité voor Economische Samenwerking (National Committee for Economic Cooperation) was created, which unified in one organization the Dutch employers with compulsory membership.[134]

Belgium: From Military Administration to (Late) Reichskommissariat

The German occupation of Belgium was marked by the flight of the democratic government into exile in France and then to the United Kingdom, with King Leopold III deciding to stay in Brussels despite the government's decision. The king tried, albeit unsuccessfully, to propose a collaborationist government to Hitler, which was rejected, and he remained locked in his palace during the war. Despite Hitler's possible intentions to create an occupation administration on the Reichskommissariat model, as in the neighboring Netherlands and several other occupied countries, Belgium and some territories in northern France remained under the control of a military administration headed by Prussian general Alexander von Falkenhausen, a reactionary military man, former member of the German Nationalist Party (Deutschnationale Volkspartei) and member of its paramilitary organization, the Stahlhelm, who later joined the Nazi Party. As Werner Warmbrunn pointed out, "what makes the Belgian case so special is that despite Hitler's original intention the final imposition of a civilian regime did not occur until July 1944, only a few weeks before the end of the occupation," when General von Falkenhausen officially transferred his

---

[133] Warmbrunn, *The Dutch under German Occupation*, pp. 136–139.
[134] David Barnouw and Jan Nekkers, "The Netherlands: State corporatism against the state," in Wyn Grant, Jan Nekkers and Frans van Waarden, eds., *Organising Business for War. Corporatist Economic Organisation during the Second World War*, Oxford, Berg, 1991, p. 151.

authority to the former Gauleiter of Cologne, Josep Grohe.[135] However, the tensions between the military administration and the political institutions of the Nazi "polyocracy" (together with the corresponding specter of a change in the type of administration) were always present, conditioning the military authorities and the strategies of the local collaborationists.[136]

In the process of fleeing Brussels, the Belgian coalition government left the administration to the Secretaries-General of the Ministries – it would be the Council of Secretaries-General who constituted a quasi-government under occupation. It would be they, together with some new structures created by the German military administration, who would run Belgium, producing legislation, albeit under previous German control. Needless to say, all elected federal, regional, and local political institutions were dissolved, electoral procedures suspended, and administrative authority strengthened. On the other hand, the occupying authorities also created commissariats with a clear pre-corporatist structure, like the Commissariats for Reconstruction, Wages, and Prices; for Provincial and Communal Finances; and others which went beyond the structures of the ministries.

The military administration considered itself the supervisory body, but its interference and veto power was great, "even if it remains true that in Belgium existing government services were left more scope and autonomy than in the Netherlands."[137] Progressively, however, Party agencies and the SS settled in Belgium, starting to interfere in specific programs and developing their relationship with the parties, elites, and repressive institutions. The SS-Gruppenführer Eggert Reeder, a civilian administrator under von Falkenhausen, quickly became the Belgian administration's interlocutor in the political and economic spheres.

Most of the Belgian political parties were illegalized and some self-dissolved by their own initiative, such as the Parti ouvrier belge (POB) of Hendrik de Man, a revisionist socialist who embraced corporatism and collaboration after the occupation. The two most important parties that tried profit from the critical juncture of the occupation and get closer to power were Leon Degrelle's Rexist Party and the Flemish National League (VNV).

The Rexist Party was born in the early 1930s as a radical right-wing party very much characterized by authoritarian and corporatist political

---

[135] Werner Warmbrunn, *The German Occupation of Belgium, 1940–1944*, New York, Peter Lang, 1993, p. 96.
[136] See Jay Howard Geller, "The role of military administration in German-occupied Belgium, 1940–1944," *The Journal of Military History*, 63, no. 1 (January 1999), pp. 99–125.
[137] Warmbrunn, *The German Occupation of Belgium*, p. 70.

Catholicism, modeled on Dolfuss's Austria and Salazar's Portugal, and later progressively acquiring a more "clerical-fascist" structure and ideology.[138] Although it had a national organizational structure, its political base never went beyond Wallonia and Brussels. Its most significant electoral result came in the 1936 general election, when it won 11.49 percent and then reached a political agreement with the VNV. The VNV got 7.1 percent, but was to grow electorally in Flanders with its authoritarian program of federation with the Netherlands, unlike Rex. Both parties coalesced around the political project of an authoritarian and corporatist Belgium, but the agreement was short-lived.[139] Although their aspirations for power were quickly moderated by the military administration, these remained the only two authorized parties.

Before these parties had a monopoly on political action in occupied Belgium, between the eve of and the first months of the occupation, several projects to establish an authoritarian regime and a single party failed due to vetoes by the occupying authorities and Hitler himself. The first, with a programmatic draft written by Henri de Man at the request of King Leopold III and sponsored by the Royal Court, had as its program the "consolidation of the constitutional monarchy" and "constitution of a government temporarily responsible for all legislative and executive power" by means of a plebiscite, the "replacement of the Chambers by consultative institutions on a corporatist basis," and the "abolition of parties replaced by a single party."[140] Part of this project would involve the new constitution requested by the King, and one of the project's authors, Henri Velge (an eminent jurist with prominent positions at Catholic employers' associations) proposed a "royal dictatorship": All powers, except those expressly assigned to other bodies by the Constitution or by law, belonged to the king. The king exercised legislative and executive powers. The Houses were replaced by General-Estates elected on a corporatist basis, with no right of legislative initiative or interpellation, and the ministers were only accountable to the king.[141]

---

[138] See Martin Conway, *Collaboration in Belgium. Léon Degrelle and the Rexist Movement, 1940–1044*, New Haven, CT, Yale University Press, 1993.

[139] See Giovanni Cappocia, *Defending Democracy. Reactions to Extremism in Interwar Europe*, Baltimore, MD, The Johns Hopkins University Press, 2005, p. 109.

[140] Cited in Eric-Johri Nachtergaele, "Les relations Léopold ll – Henri De Man (1938–1940)," *Res Publica*, 1 (1978), p. 34.

[141] Françoise Miller, "Henri Velge, l'artisan du Conseil d'Etat belge (1911–1946)," *Revue Belge d'Histoire Contemporaine* XXXVII, no. 1–2 (2007), p. 165. According to Dirk Luyton, in 1940, "Velge's corporatism had a dual structure and was a mixture of Italian fascist and Nazi corporatism." See Dirk Luyten and Rik Hemmerijckx, "Belgian labour

Another failed project was that of the creation of a single party. Both Rex and the VNV made agreements for its creation and some Catholic conservative journalists, such as Robert Poulet and Raymond De Becker, rehearsed in 1941 the creation of a single party that would be broader than the fascist initiatives. Under the name "Parti des Provinces Romanes," its program was aimed at the "construction of a federal Belgian state based on authoritarian and corporatist principles."[142] With its statutes signed by leading figures in the collaboration, Leon Degrelle distanced himself from the initiative, but in any case, the German military administration informed the organizers that the creation of the party was premature and would not be authorized. The decision was made public, also stating that only Rex and the VNV would have legal space in occupied Belgium.[143] Blocking the creation of an authoritarian regime and a single party closed off the opportunity for the institutionalization of a collaborationist dictatorship based on political corporatism, so popular with segments of Belgian conservatism and the radical right.[144]

Between Belgian collaboration and the will of the occupier, nevertheless, social corporatism would quickly be introduced.[145] In the employers' field, it suffered some resistance (which was more practical than ideological), and in the trade union field, it had the collaboration of several union confederations and important segments of their leading elite. Although supervised by the so-called Dienststelle Hellwig, made up of staff from the German Labor Front and created within the Military Administration in October 1940, the native component was initially very significant in institutionalizing social corporatism. In fact, with some pre-emption from the Belgian side and German initiative, "the Secretaries-General and businessmen created the corporatist organisations themselves within a framework imposed by the German occupier."[146]

---

in World War II: Strategies of survival, organisations and labour relations," *European Review of History: Revue européenne d'histoire*, 7, no. 2 (2002), p. 218.

[142] Conway, *Collaboration in Belgium*, p. 86. On Raymond de Becker, see Olivier Dard, Etienne Deschamps, and Genevieve Duchenne. *Raymond de Becker (1912–1969): Itineraire et Facettes d'un Intellectuel Reprouvé*, Bruxelles, P.I.E.-Peter Lang, 2013.

[143] Conway, *Collaboration in Belgium*, p. 87

[144] On the projects of political corporatism in Belgium, see the important works of Dirk Luyten, especially "Politiek corporatisme em de crisis van de liberale ideologien (1920–1944)," *Belgisch Tijdschrift voor Nieuwste Geschiedenis*, 1–2, Deel 2 (1993), pp. 107–184.

[145] See Kenneth Bertrams and Sabine Rudischhauser, "German Ambitions and Belgian Expectations: Social Insurance and Industrial Relations in Occupied Belgium, 1940–1944," in Kott and Patel, eds., *Nazism across Borders*, pp. 389–417.

[146] Dirk Luyton, "The 'Policy of the Lesser Evil': Corporatist Economic Organisation in Belgium," in Grant, Nekkers and Waarden, eds., *Organising Business for War*, p. 174.

In a manifesto, Henri de Man called for the unification of the trade union confederations along corporatist lines, and the Catholic, Socialist, and Liberal confederations responded positively to this call. The association between trade unions and employers' associations with the three dominant political families before the occupation, and the great ideological penetration of corporatism into them, meant that the Catholics in particular welcomed the abolition of the "class struggle" and the "immediate establishment of a corporatist regime."[147] In November 1940, not without some resistance, the Union of Manual and Intellectual Workers (Union des Travailleurs Manuels et Intellectuels; UTMI) was created, headed by a board of the four former trade union confederations associated with the political parties, with particular emphasis on the Catholic and Socialist parties, but also including the Flemish trade union sector of the VNV, the Labor Order (Arbeidsorde). Shortly afterwards, the old leadership was removed and the UTMI was given a new leader in 1941 with the appointment of Edgar Delvo, a former associate of Henri De Man who came from the VNV and the Arbeidsorde (well-known for their corporatist proposals in the 1930s, but which had radicalized toward fascism in 1940). In 1942, the dissolution of the old trade unions was decreed, some of which would remain underground. This process was completed with the decree of August 26, 1942 which provided for the formal dissolution of the old unions and for legal transfer of their assets to the UTMI.[148]

In the case of the agricultural world, which was very important for the war economy, the German administration asked the Council of Secretaries-General to set up the Department for Agriculture and Food Control (Département de l'Agriculture et du Ravitaillement) and the creation of the state-controlled and compulsory National Corporation for Agriculture and Food Supply (Corporation Nationale de L'Agriculture et de l'Alimentation; CNAA) was quick.[149]

The corporatist UTMI was weak compared to the powerful employers' confederation, the Central Industrial Committee (Comité Central Industriel; CCI), to which were added other problems marked by the Wallonie-Flanders cleavage and by those associated with various political families, particularly the Catholic one. In addition, the employers'

---

[147] José Gotovich, "Belgique: Église et syndicats sous l'occupation 1940–1942 (note documentaire)," *Revue du Nord*, 60, no. 238, (July–September 1978), p. 582.

[148] See Luyten and Hemmerijckx, "Belgian labour in World War II," pp. 207–227.

[149] See Dirk Luyten, "The Belgian business elite, economic exploitation and national socialist corporatism," in Harold James and Jakob Tanner, eds., *Enterprise in the Period of Fascism in Europe*, London, Ashgate, 2003, p. 214.

associations had already been influenced by Catholic corporatist models and Italian Fascism since the 1930s. Despite German pressure for them to join joint committees with the UTMI, the CCI avoided them even though it was part of the "works councils" and other structures at the company level, following the German model. For labor relations, a new institution was created: the Committees of Social Experts, found in each economic sector and composed of representatives of the UTMI and employers' associations. Another institution was the Statutory Trade Organization, created in 1941 "as an all-embracing organisational framework for industry, commerce, and handicrafts."[150]

If initially the German military administration kept some distance from Rex and the Flemish VNV, these parties rapidly became the central players of collaboration (with the Flemish VNV predominating), in many cases rivaling each other in the political and administrative positions offered by the German administration, in collaboration with the SS, in anti-Semitic propaganda, and in the deportation of Jewish communities to extermination camps from 1942 onwards. Both Degrelle's REX and the VNV grew in the corporatist bodies and in the local administration, despite the fact that the German military administration never acceded to their wishes to be given more political power, especially relevant for Degrelle, not least because the REX had a weak organization.[151] The VNV elite achieved more, especially with the appointment of Victor Leemans as Secretary-General for Economic Affairs, with various technocrats in key posts and also in the local administration.[152] Trying to gain ground by the potential power increase of the SS and Nazi Party agencies in the event of a possible replacement by a Reichskommissariat, these parties could already do little when it finally arrived just a few weeks before the Allied armies entered Belgium.

The Baltic Countries: "Self-administrations" and "à la Slovakia" Temptations

Shortly before the Soviet occupation, in 1940, the three Baltic countries were dominated by right-wing dictatorships, some with consolidating corporatist institutions.[153] After independence and democratization in the

---

[150] Luyton, "The 'Policy of the Lesser Evil': Corporatist Economic Organisation in Belgium," p. 168.
[151] Conway, *Collaboration in Belgium*, p. 144.
[152] See Nico Wouters, *Mayoral Collaboration under Nazi Occupation in Belgium, the Netherlands and France, 1938–46*, London, Palgrave, 2016.
[153] Andres Kasekamp, "Corporatism and authoritarianism in the Baltics: Päts'Estonia in comparison," in Pinto, ed., *Corporatism and Fascism*, pp. 257–271.

early 1920s, the construction of personalized authoritarian regimes in the young Baltic countries was rapid. In 1926, a military coup in Lithuania brought Antanas Smetona to power, while in 1934 an almost syncretic series of coups led to the institutionalization of presidentialist dictatorships in Estonia and Latvia, which were only brought to an end with the Soviet invasion in 1940. The most elaborate attempts to institutionalize corporatist regimes in the region took place under Konstantin Päts in Estonia and Karlis Ulmanis in Latvia. Occupied and integrated into the Soviet Union, the Baltic countries were again occupied, this time by Nazi Germany, just a year later in 1941.

Despite some initial attempts by native authoritarian elites to establish collaborationist political regimes, with promises of liberation from Soviet domination and a return to independence, and some military commanders contemplating models closer to these, Nazi Germany established in 1941 the Reichskommissariat Ostland with headquarters in Riga to administer Estonia, Latvia, Lithuania, Belarus, and eastern Poland.[154] Each became a Generalbezirk (Main District) named after the respective country, administered by a Generalkommissar (Commissioner-General). The Reichskommissariat Ostland depended on the newly created Reich Ministry for the Occupied Eastern Territories (Reichsministerium für die besetzten Ostgebiete or Ostministerium) directed by Alfred Rosenberg (not coincidentally, a Baltic German), and led from Riga by Reichskommissar Hinrich Lohse, a former Gauleiter of Schleswig-Holstein. As Dallin notes, this decision by Hitler "on the surface ... marked a setback for the competing agencies and rival leaders. In reality Rosenberg's appointment solved none of the budding conflicts ... and disagreement was clearly apparent over the three interlocking problems of basic policy, jurisdiction of competing agencies, and personnel."[155]

For Rosenberg, the Baltics were considered a "territory for German settlement," and the Estonians especially were seen with sympathy by the German Nazi elite, but initial moves to restore previous authoritarian elites from the independence period were nevertheless blocked.[156] In Lithuania, a clandestine Lithuanian Activists' Front (LAF) took power one day after the German invasion, announcing the "establishment of

---

[154] See Sebastian Lehmann, Robert Bohn and Uwe Danker, eds., *Reichskommissariat Ostland: Tatort und Erinnerungsobjekt, Konstruktionen*, Paderborn, Ferdinand Schöningh, 2012.

[155] Alexander Dallin, *German Rule in Russia, 1941–1945: A Study of Occupation Policies*, Boulder, Westview Press, 1981, p. 84.

[156] Cited in Dallin, *German Rule in Russia*, p. 184.

a provisional government which would restore the institutions of the pre-war republic."[157] Initially tolerated, it would be disbanded six weeks later. In Latvia, insurgents proclaimed their liberation from Soviet occupation and the formation of a provisional government as well, but a German-led "self-government" was nonetheless installed. In Tallin, Jüri Uluots, the last Prime Minister of independent Estonia, proposed a "domestic administrative center," which was rejected as well.[158]

The "self-governments" that the Reichskommissariat Ostland installed in the three Baltic countries were of a hybrid structure, recruiting from segments of the political class of previous authoritarian regimes and marked by political distrust of their autonomist projects. Formally administered by German Generalkommissars, they controlled a native self-administration (landeseigene Verwaltung) headed by a directorate (or council in Lithuania), with structures equivalent to ministries, such as education, social security, or economy. These ministry-equivalents, which ranged in number from five to twelve, were headed by "Country Directors" (Landesdirektoren) in Estonia, "General Directors" (Generaldirektoren) in Latvia, and "General Counselors" (Generalräte) in Lithuania. Although formally with administrative and advisory functions, their First Directors (Erster Direktor) or First General Counselors (Erster Generalrat) were in many cases politicians and not bureaucrats coming from the state administrative apparatus.[159] As we will see, both for strategic reasons and due to genuine "polyocratic" indecision, the eventual evolution toward a more autonomous government was sometimes postponed and sometimes blocked.

For the leadership of these native "self-administrations," political figures associated with authoritarian regimes prior to the Soviet invasion were chosen, some even more to the right of them. This would be the case of General Petras Kubiliunas, a Lithuanian military man who even participated in a fascistic coup d'état against Smetona led by another dissident, Augustinas Voldemaras. The other two had taken refuge in Germany after the Soviet occupation and returned to their countries directly from there to head their "self-administrations," such as General Oskars Dankers in Latvia and Hjalmar Mäe in Estonia. The former suffered some

---

[157] Andres Kasekamp, *A History of the Baltic States*, London, Palgrave, 2010, p. 132.
[158] Kari Alenius, "Balancing between dissent and conformity: Estonian self-administration under German occupation, 1941–1944," *Revista Română de Studii Baltice și Nordice / The Romanian Journal for Baltic and Nordic Studies*, 11, no. 1 (2019), p. 59.
[159] Romuald J. Misiunas and Rein Taagepera, *The Baltic States. Years of Dependence, 1940–1990*, Berkeley, The University of California Press, 1993, p. 51.

mistrust and found it difficult to assert himself in the face of the projects of collaborationist governments that emerged immediately in Riga. The second, Hjalmar Mäe, was an Estonian politician who evolved to the extreme right and to a fascism associated with the Vaps movement, of which he was a propaganda strategist.[160] Other members of the former authoritarian elite filled prominent posts and some managed to transition from the provisional governments after the Soviet withdrawal to the new "self-government" imposed by the German occupation. Alfred Valdmanis, for example, one of the most prominent politicians in Latvia in the 1930s, was regarded with suspicion by some segments of the German occupation elite, who saw him as a frontman for the "Ulmanis clique."[161] A participant from the first hour in the negotiations with the German authorities, and initially refusing the leadership of General Oskars Dankers, Valdemanis would be Director of Justice for a time and was almost to replace Dankers.[162] Alberts Kviesis, who was President of the Republic of Latvia, also served in self-government as head of a Directorate for a time. Without control of Riga, directly administered by the German occupiers, distrust of self-government was great and contradictory, so much so that "The directors general ... were not to be considered a collegial body – the term 'directorate general' was to be avoided – but individually responsible to the Generalkommissar."[163] Elements closer to fascism, such as some former Vaps or Perkonkrusts (Thundercross), banned by previous dictatorial regimes, also emerged in collaboration, especially in police and militia institutions.[164] However, when in 1942 Rosenberg approved the list of directors general of Latvia he "endorsed Drechsler's criteria for the selection – professional qualifications, political reliability, and respect among the Latvian population."[165] These principles had apparently been applied to the rest of the Baltic neighbors.

The tension between strict German control and some room for maneuver of these "self-governments" was always present. They went through phases of greater autonomy or greater repression, also passing through

---

[160] Andres Kasekamp, *The Radical Right in Interwar Estonia*, London, Palgrave, 2000, p. 59. See also from the same author, "Fascism by Popular Initiative: The Rise and Fall of the Vaps Movement in Estonia," *Fascism*, 4 (2015), pp. 155–168.

[161] Gerhard P. Bassler, *Alfred Valdmanis and the Politics of Survival*, Toronto, The University of Toronto Press, 2000, p. 116.

[162] Bassler, *Alfred Valdmanis and the Politics of Survival*, pp. 121–122.

[163] Bassler, *Alfred Valdmanis and the Politics of Survival*, p. 124.

[164] See Matthew Kott, "Latvia's *Pērkonkrusts*: Anti-German National Socialism in a Fascistogenic Milieu," *Fascism*, 4 (2015), pp. 169–193.

[165] Cited in Bassler, *Alfred Valdmanis and the Politics of Survival*, p. 125.

the removal and detention of directors. The impact of Nazi "polyocracy" present in many other occupied territories was felt in the Baltics as well, with power distributed among several Nazi political and economic institutions.[166] One of the main claims of the "self-governments" – the re-privatization of property nationalized by the Soviet occupation – was not done, except in some modest experiments from 1943 on, with the German occupying forces taking the administration of all industry and communications infrastructures. One field where collaboration was significant was in the area of security and the war effort. Combining nationalist sentiments with anti-communism, the Waffen SS and other paramilitary organizations experienced greater recruitment success in the Baltic States than other areas of occupied Europe, albeit with many conscripts. Although in a more diversified way, collaboration in the dynamics of the Holocaust was also significant.[167] Initially localized, with the formation of the Reichskommissariat Ostland and the presence of the SS, the formal and informal development of anti-Jewish measures, massacres, and executions immediately grew, fulfilling one of the most coherent ideological goals of German National Socialism.

The regime-building projects of the collaborationist Baltic politicians, although they had arisen and sometimes been accepted by some institutions of the occupying power, did not succeed, despite the fact that the example of Slovakia appeared several times. Leading figures in the Estonian and Latvian directorates, like Oskar Angelus and Alfreds Valdmanis, wrote memoranda with such plans, but were opposed by Reichskommissar Lohse. Otto Drechsler, the German General Commissioner for Latvia, although rejecting it before Valdmanis, opened the process confidentially, suggesting at the end of 1942 "autonomy along Slovakian or at least Bohemian-Moravian lines."[168] Karl Litzmann, the German Commissioner for Estonia, "also supported Slovakian-type autonomy."[169] In 1943 Rosenberg himself wrote a proposal to Hitler on the three Baltic states, including the rapid restoration of private property and the creation of autonomous governments, but

---

[166] See Dallin, *German Rule in Russia*, pp. 193–197, and on Latvia, Valdis o. Lumans, *Latvia in World War Two*, New York, Fordham University Press, 2006, pp. 173–209.
[167] See Matthew Kott, Arūnas Bubnys, and Ülle Kraft, "The Baltic States. Auxiliaries and Waffen-SS soldiers from Estonia, Latvia, and Lithuania," in Jochen Böhler and Robert Gerwarth, eds., *The Waffen-SS. A European History*, Oxford, Oxford University Press, 2017, pp. 120–164.
[168] Misiunas and Taagepera, *The Baltic States*, p. 67.
[169] Misiunas and Taagepera, *The Baltic States*, p. 68.

"met Hitler's uncompromising veto."[170] According to Rosenberg's proposal, Lithuania, Latvia, and Estonia would become "state entities" under the "protection" of the Reich, responsible for military and foreign affairs and dissolving the Reichskommissariat Ostland.[171] At the same time, the German mayor of Riga, Hugo Wittrock, in a report to Rosenberg, wrote suspiciously, "First Volkshilfe, then directorate general, now protectorate, then 'à la Slovakia,' and finally merely a loose treaty with the Reich. The end – I don't want to spell out!"[172]

4 Japan's "Greater East Asia Co-Prosperity Sphere" and Its Occupation Regimes

Japan's political change in the 1930s integrated it into the broader global autocratic wave during the Era of Fascism, aligning it with the Axis powers through the Tripartite Pact and its participation in World War II alongside Nazi Germany and Fascist Italy.[173]

The transition to authoritarianism in Japan coincided with imperialist expansion and war in Asia, accompanied by increased military intervention in political institutions. In the context of a rapidly changing international environment, which included imperialist expansion in Southeast Asia, alignment with the Axis powers, and war, Prince Konoe Fumimaro's "New Order" reforms represented a significant effort to establish a dictatorial single-party system rooted in the institutionalization of political and social corporatism.[174] While the latter was largely realized, the former, as in several other dictatorships of the fascist era, was only partially implemented.[175] Despite its strong ideological roots in the conservative Japanese political culture, the diffusion of Italian and German fascist models was important in the reforms designed by the main intellectual-politicians of the regime.[176] Moreover, it also formed the foundation of economic and social policy in the areas under Japanese occupation.

---

[170] Misiunas and Taagepera, *The Baltic States*, p. 67.
[171] Cited in Dallin, *German Rule in Russia*, p. 194.
[172] Bassler, *Alfred Valdmanis and the Politics of Survival*, p. 153.
[173] See Hedinger, *Die Achse Berlin-Rom-Tokio 1919–1946*.
[174] See Gordon Mark Berger, *Parties Out of Power in Japan. 1931–1941*, Princeton, NJ, Princeton University Press, 1977.
[175] See Sheldon Garon, *The State and Labor in Modern Japan*, Berkeley, University of California Press, 1987.
[176] William Miles Fletcher III, *The Search for a New Order: Intellectuals and Fascism in Prewar Japan*, Chapell Hill, University of North Carolina Press, 1982; Reto Hofmann, *The Fascist Effect: Japan and Italy, 1915–1952*, Ithaca, NY, and London, Cornell University Press, 2015.

The debate surrounding the classification of the Japanese dictatorship has been rich, ranging from such categorizations as "emperor-system fascism" to "corporatist dictatorship," "military–bureaucratic regime," and "military authoritarianism," and even encompassing definitions like "fascist imperialist" and "techno-fascism."[177] While some of these classifications emphasize specific aspects, notably "the fusion of fascism and imperialism,"[178] the prominent role played by the armed forces in the transition toward authoritarianism, coupled with imperialist endeavors, the gradual and elitist nature of the transition, and the simultaneous presence of radicalization and total war within a framework of conservative authoritarianism, have rendered dictatorial Japan a particularly challenging case for comparison. In fact, the most salient feature of Authoritarian Japan was its gradual institutionalization and the persistence of a "limited pluralism," which hindered the complete consolidation of a single-party regime from above, with new authoritarian structures supplanting parliamentary and (semi-)democratic systems. However, the progressive dominance of the armed forces over the regime does have some singularity because they are intertwined in all authoritarian institutions, from the government to the single party, the militia and propaganda organizations, from corporatist institutions to economic ones. Like a precocious version of "bureaucratic authoritarianism," this model of military intervention, without a unified and personalized leadership, was less present in other regimes. It ended up enshrining a system of "diffused political responsibility" that marked the entire duration of the regime until its military defeat in 1945.[179]

The creation of collaborationist dictatorships under military occupation was also a hallmark of the Japanese pole of the Axis, and in addition to the "Model State" of Manchukuo, it included the Wang Jinwei regime in China, the "Second Philippine Republic," the "State of Burma," and even the curious "Provisional Government of Free India," headed from Singapore by the veteran Indian nationalist Chandra Bose.[180]

---

[177] see Federico Marcon's, "The quest for Japanese fascism: A historiographical overview," in Giovanni Bulian and Silvia Rivadossi, eds., *Itineraries of an Anthropologist: Studies in Honour of Massimo Raveri*, Venice, Ca 'Foscari Edizione, 2021, pp. 53–86.

[178] Hofmann, *The Fascist Effect*, p. 33.

[179] Berger *Parties Out*, p. 296. See Peter Wetzler, *Hirohito and War: Imperial Tradition and Military Decision Making in Prewar Japan*, Honolulu, University of Hawaii Press, 1998.

[180] The "Provisional Government of Free India," recognized by some Axis powers, was also established by Japan in Singapore, in 1943, lead by the Indian nationalist Chandra Bose. Bose had fascinating political and ideological relations with Nazi Germany and the Axis, but will not be discussed here. There is an extensive bibliography on the topic. Vide Marzia Casolari, *The Shadow of the Swastika. The Relationships between Indian Radical Nationalism, Italian Fascism and Nazism*, London, Routledge, 2020.

As in occupied Europe, some were truly native regimes (such as that of Thailand), but in the case of Burma and the Philippines, they were a construction of the occupier with the collaboration of local nationalist elites. Both Burma and the Philippines were under Western colonial rule (but with promises of independence since the 1930s, some with a date set) when the Japanese Armed Forces arrived. Prospects of independence, associated with representative liberal democratic institutions, were then replaced by the creation of authoritarian "Independent States" under Japanese rule.

Japan's colonial expansion in East Asia preceded World War II, but its transition to authoritarianism in the 1930s was inextricably linked to an imperialist step forward and to the growing pro-authoritarian intervention of the Japanese Armed Forces in the political system. This institutional dimension was less present in the European poles of the Axis. Although by definition the Italian and German Armed Forces were important players in the political models of military occupation, they were less decisive in shaping the types of occupation and political regimes implemented locally.[181] In the case of Japan, on the other hand, although fragmented, they always had a decisive role in the strategy for occupying and administering the occupied territories, sometimes in a tense manner. However, the very structure and locus of political decision-making in Authoritarian Japan reflected the great weight and autonomy of the military elite, progressively diverted from the government to the so-called, "Liaison conference" between the Government and the Imperial General Headquarters (IGHQ) under the supervision of the Emperor, a structure dominated by the Armed Forces which became "Japan's *de facto* war cabinet."[182] As in the case of National Socialism and Italian Fascism, the dynamics of occupation followed in some cases a strategy that was intended to be a permanent, and in others which was more linked to the vicissitudes of the war, but despite several projects designed by Japanese strategists and ideologues, it is difficult to find great coherence. As some historians have noticed, Japanese "'plurality of imperial rule' does not reflect a well-thought-out master plan, but a mishmash of improvised measures and prolonged disputes about

---

[181] See David Rodogno, "Wartime occupation by Italy," in Richard Bosworth and Joseph Maiolo, eds., *The Cambridge History of the Second World War*. Vol. 2, *Politics and Ideology*, Cambridge, Cambridge University Press, 2015, pp. 436–458; Fonzi, *Altro I Confini*, pp. 45–61.

[182] See Jeremy A. Yellen, "What grand strategy? Japan, 1931–1945," in Brian P. Farrell, S. R. Joey Long and David J. Ulbrich, eds., *From Far East to Asia Pacific. Great Powers and Grand Strategy 1900–1954*, Berlin, De Gruyter, 2022, p. 249.

authority and direction that lasted until the last days of the war."[183] The objective of economic and political domination in the service of the war and Japan was naturally always present, but here a mark of "liberation" from European colonialism went hand in hand with economic and labor exploitation.

The building of the so-called "Greater East Asia Co-Prosperity Sphere," the basis for the ideological and political legitimation of Japanese imperialist expansion, was very well summarized by Ethan Mark as being that of a "strident rejection of Western culture and institutions and the embracing of an imagined Asian-Japanese alternate modernity."[184] This new authoritarian modernity was associated with the "belief that Japan's world-historic, divine national mission as a nation was to lead and liberate Asia," "in favor of a 'return' to a harmonious social order combining the best of 'old' and 'new'; 'classless' social corporatism; racial, cultural, and gender essentialism; military expansion; and a rejection of 'Anglo-American' hegemony (that) was in many ways reminiscent of the national socialist or fascist trends triumphant in Italy and Germany, but also present in many other places in the same period."[185] Regardless of the type of institutions and regimes of occupation, the common model, disseminated and attempted to be built by the political and propaganda apparatuses associated with military administrations, pointed to a mobilization that "represented a revolutionary intersection between state and society, driven by a convergence between the practical exigencies of modern war, crisis in the imperial order, the appeal of the fascist-social corporatist model, the radical potentials of new media techniques and technologies, and social change in a context of maturing industrial capitalism."[186]

Although in the case of Japan, the creation (or recognition) of dictatorial political regimes of collaboration was only an option adopted for some countries, it was within the institutional framework of the Greater East Asia Co-Prosperity Sphere that some new formally independent states were recognized by the Axis, like Burma and the Philippines.

---

[183] Daniel Hedinger and Moritz von Brescius, "The German and Japanese empires. Great power competition and the world wars in trans- Imperial perspective," in Peter Fibiger Bang, C. A. Bayly, and Walter Scheidel, eds., *The Oxford World History of Empire*, vol. 2, Oxford, Oxford University Press, 2021, p. 1150.

[184] Ethan Mark, *Japan's Occupation of Java in the Second World War: A Transnational History*, London, Bloomsbury, 2018, p. 18.

[185] Mark, *Japan's Occupation of Java in the Second World War*, p. 18.

[186] Mark, *Japan's Occupation of Java in the Second World War*, pp. 53–54.

In 1941, the Japanese Army and Navy divided between themselves the military administration of occupied Southeast Asia.[187] The guidelines on the "Administration of Occupied Areas" issued by the General Headquarters-Government Liaison Conference in November 1941, defined Japan's main objectives: "rapid acquisition of important defense resources" and the "securing of self-sustenance of operating military forces in the field," underlining the fact that "existing government structures are to be used to the utmost ... and former government organizations and folk customs are to be respected."[188] The political administration of the territories militarily occupied by Japan – both the old ones, such as Korea (1895) or Taiwan (1910), and those that were occupied in the meantime – had great diversity. Although in the case of older occupations a more classical colonial model was imposed, dominated by "General-Governors" and aimed at greater integration in Japan itself, the model of direct occupation with military administrations marked several territories occupied during the war. Malaya, Singapore, Java, and other territories, although with the significant participation of local nationalist elites, "were to remain as dependent parts of the empire as directly controlled territories."[189] Despite the rhetoric of "liberation" from Western colonialism, which has led some scholars to speak of the "Greater East Asia Co-Prosperity Sphere" as an "imperialism without colonies," the model of creating collaborationist, formally independent dictatorships was not generalized.[190]

In the case of Dutch Indonesia and other territories, the occupying forces divided them into several parts, with Sumatra administered jointly with the Malay peninsula, and Java with another military administration.[191] From the beginning, the nationalist elites played an important role in collaboration, both in the administration and in the vast fabric of military, economic, and labor-associated organizations created by the Japanese. Independence was not programmed, giving way to a hybrid model of administration with the participation of nationalists such as Sukarno and others. As in all areas under

---

[187] See the description of the areas at stake in Frank N. Trager, ed., *Burma: Japanese Military Administration, Selected Documents, 1941–1945*, Philadelphia, The University of Pennsylvania Press, 1971, p. 35.

[188] Cited in Gregg Huff, *World War II and Southeast Asia: Economy and Society Under Japanese Occupation*, Cambridge, Cambridge University Press, 2020, p. 56.

[189] Jeremy Yellen, *The Greater East Asia Co-Prosperity Sphere: When Total Empire Met Total War*, Ithaca, NY, Cornell University Press, 2019, p. 19.

[190] Peter Duus, "Imperialism without colonies: The vision of a greater East Asia co-prosperity sphere," *Diplomacy and Statecraft*, 7, no. 1 (1996), p. 70.

[191] See Harry J. Benda, James K. Irikura and Koichi Kish, eds., *Japanese Military Administration in Indonesia: Selected Documents*, New Haven, CT, Southeast Asia Studies, Yale University, 1965.

Japanese rule, Japanese military administrations closed the legislature, imposed censorship, and banned political parties and independent political activity, undoing the plans for an autonomous government of a group of nationalists, who even drafted a constitution.[192] The Military Administration created a "Central Advisory Council" with a significant nationalist participation, promoted major propaganda campaigns with an important number of Japanese and local cadres, and created several mass organizations in Java with "a clear parallel between these organisations and the National Spiritual Mobilisation Movement, the National Mobilisation Movement, and the Imperial Rule Assistance Association (IRAA) in Japan."[193] The same happened with political parties, with the Military Administration trying to create a single party based on the unification of local nationalist groups. This experience, not always successful, continued with the creation of the Triple A Movement, replaced by the Center of the People's Spiritual Power (Putera), led by Sukarno and Mohammad Hatta, and succeeded by the highly controlled "Java Service Association," modeled on the IRAA.[194]

In French Indochina and Thailand, the options were diverse. In the first case Japan kept the French administration (which was obedient to the Vichy Regime) a dependent ally of the Axis, which was pursuing a corporatist "national revolution" under colonial rule in Indochina. In the second case, the Japanese occupation kept in power the previous government, which became a collaborationist regime that quickly declared war on the Allies. French Indochina was led by a governor loyal to the Vichy Regime, Vice Admiral Jean Decoux, who, from 1940 onwards, reorganized the colonial institutions along corporatist lines, inaugurating a cult of Marshal Pétain.[195] Between ultimatums and the mediation of Nazi Germany, Japanese forces occupied much of the territory, maintaining the French administration and even its colonial Armed Forces until almost the end of the war in 1945, when they dissolved and imprisoned them before the advance of Allied forces in Europe, fearing that this colonial administration would change sides.

---

[192] David Bourchier, *Illiberal Democracy in Indonesia. The Ideology of the Family State*, London, Routledge, 2015, p. 51.

[193] Shigeru Sato, *War, Nationalism and Peasants Java under the Japanese Occupation 1942–1945*, Armonk, NY, M. E. Sharp, 1994, p. 20. See also the chapter "Corporatism in the service of Japan's War," in Bourchier, *Illiberal Democracy in Indonesia*, pp. 51–55.

[194] See Sven Matthiessen, "Re-orienting the Philippines: The KALIBAPI party and the application of Japanese Pan-Asianism, 1942–45," *Modern Asian Studies* 53, no. 2, 2019, p. 567.

[195] See a table with the new corporatist governing structure in the excellent study of Sébastien Verney, *L'Indochine sous Vichy. Entre Révolution nationale, collaboration et identités nationales 1940–1945*, Paris, Riveneuve éditions, 2012, pp. 11 and 211.

When Japan invaded Thailand in 1941, this independent and internationally recognized state was already dominated by an authoritarian regime controlled by military and conservative civilians, who in 1932 carried out a coup against the monarch, leaving the king with fewer powers. Headed by Plaek Phibunsongkhram, better known as Phibun, assisted by his rival Pridi Phanomyong, an intellectual-politician who would become Minister of Foreign Affairs, and Luang Wichit Wathakan, his "chief-ideologue," this quasi-dictator remained in power from 1938 until 1944.[196] A military veteran involved in both political and military conspiracies, progressively more authoritarian in his views, and an admirer of the dictatorships of the Era of Fascism, between 1934 and 1936, Phibun "openly called for dictatorship, claiming that the licentious creed of democracy would lead the country to disaster."[197] While maintaining the monarchy, Phibun associated the project of building a modern nation with that of building a strong and interventionist state – and with his personalized leadership, which was a true "cult of personality," "influenced by the modern ideology of European fascism."[198] As an editorial in the London *Times* pointed out, Phibun's constitutional and political projects suggested "that in practice and at the outset it will be a one-party Government of mildly Fascist complexion."[199] As in other dictatorships, Phibun created paramilitary youth organizations, like the Yuwachon (for males) and Yuwanari (for girls), censored the press, and controlled the radio, being also influenced by Chiang Kai-shek's New Life Movement. In December 1938, Phibun formally became his nation's leader, with his People's Party dominating the National Assembly. Parliament became practically powerless, but it was not reorganized along corporatist lines. The concentration of power under Phibun was also marked by the accumulation of ministerial portfolios and that of commander-in-chief of the army.[200] It was this regime that the Japanese invasion found and that gave them "transit rights" in their territory. Phibun quickly put Thailand into the service of Japan and the Axis, declaring war on the Allies while also obtaining

---

[196] Federico Ferrara, *The Political Development of Modern Thailand*, Cambridge, Cambridge University Press, 2015, p. 110. For a description of the main political events in this period, see E. Bruce Reynolds, *Thailand and Japan's Southern Advance, 1940–1945*, New York, S. Martin's Press, 1994.

[197] Ferrara, *The Political Development of Modern Thailand*, p. 105.

[198] Ferrara, *The Political Development of Modern Thailand*, p. 111. On how the "Elements of the model set by European fascist regimes ... were appropriated" by Phibun, see pp. 111–121.

[199] Cited in E. Bruce Reynolds, "Phibun Songkhram and Thai nationalism in the fascist era," *European Journal of East Asian Studies*, 3, no. 1 (2004), p. 103.

[200] See Reynolds, "Phibun Songkhram and Thai nationalism in the fascist era," pp. 99–134.

territorial concessions from the Japanese occupier. Although Thailand's authoritarian regime was not an institutional product of the Japanese occupation, it was nonetheless integrated into the "Greater East Asia Co-Prosperity Sphere." Japan's plans pointed to "as circumstances permit, bring[ing] about the reorganization of Thailand's economic system as a member of the Greater East Asia economic bloc."[201]

Manchukuo: The "Model State"

Created in 1931 in the Chinese province of Manchuria, the institutionalization of the "State of Manchukuo" in the following years was a mirror of the model of political regime that the most important segments of Japan's political elite wanted to associate with their imperialist expansion in Asia, in apparent synchrony with "the transition to authoritarian rule in Japan and its move to the axis with Nazi Germany and fascist Italy."[202] As Dubois stresses, Manchukuo turned into "the laboratory and showcase of Japanese developmental imperialism," becoming in the late 1930s "both the 'Jewel in the Crown' of the Japanese Empire, and a microcosm of the empire itself."[203] For some historians, "Manchukuo provided a staging ground for the development of Asianism as a constituent of (Japanese) fascist imperialism."[204] However, unlike fascist Italy, the project to create Manchukuo suffered from contradictions and tensions that marked the metropolitan power in Japan with a political system, which, although authoritarian, had only weak unified political decision-making, progressively dominated by its armed forces.

The decisive role in the creation of Manchukuo was played by the military action of the so-called Kwantung Army, a division of the Japanese army created for this purpose in the early twentieth century, which (after a false explosion attributed to China) invaded Manchuria without the consent of the authorities in Tokyo. From then on, the Kwantung Army began the political, economic, and social construction of an occupation regime with the active participation of Japanese institutions,

---

[201] Cited in William L. Swan, "Japan's intentions for its greater East Asia co-prosperity sphere as indicated in its policy plans for Thailand," *Journal of Southeast Asian Studies*, 27, no. 1 (1996), p. 142.

[202] Thomas David DuBois, "Ideology and control instruments of authoritarianism in Japanese Manchuria," in Pinto and Adnolfi, eds., *Building Dictatorships under Axis Rule*, p. 251.

[203] DuBois, "Ideology and control instruments of authoritarianism in Japanese Manchuria," p. 252.

[204] Louise Young, "When fascism met empire in Japanese-occupied Manchuria," *Journal of Global History*, 12, no. 2 (2017), p. 282.

especially when Japan invaded the rest of China from 1937 onwards. When comparing Manchukuo's institutions with other regimes of the fascist era, the "similarities include the nondemocratic and narrow circle of decision-makers, policies of state-led industrialization and modernization, implementation through a state-sponsored mass organization (the Concordia Association, Xiehehui, Kyowakat), and a corporatist system in which each group has its place and function within the state."[205]

Manchukuo's political, social, and economic institutions were designed by the Kwantung Army's general staff, with a decisive role played by authoritarian intellectual-politicians and segments of the upper bureaucratic elite of Tokyo, making it a model of authoritarian state-led modernization.[206] The circulation of ideas, projects, and models between Japan and Manchukuo, during the process of regime building without the institutional constrains of Japan itself, caused some historians to consider that Manchukuo had more fascist traits than Japan itself. In a nutshell: "The new state would have corporatism as its base, military ensuring its 'protection,' and a mass organization – the Concordia Association – to communicate its ideals to the people. It followed a utopian fascism resembling the Italian model under Mussolini in the early to mid-1930s, and, after 1937, it followed Nazi Germany's 'neo-corporatism'."[207]

Initially a republic, Manchukuo was transformed in a monarchy headed by the last emperor of China, Puyi, already its formal leader, in 1934.[208] According the "Organizational Law of the Government" of the "New State," Manchukuo was led by Puyi (who had a privy council) and by an executive branch, the General Affairs State Council, with ten ministers headed by a prime minister. If the ministers were native Chinese, they were controlled by Japanese vice ministers appointed by the Kwantung Army. More important, the Office of Administrative Affairs of the State Council was entirely controlled by the Japanese. The Legislative Council, Manchukuo's legislature, was not elected and its functions, as in many other correspondent regimes, was to "assist" the executive branch, with very limited capacity to veto Cabinet legislation. Secret agreements were also the basis of global control of Machukuo by the Japanese occupying

---

[205] Prasenjit Duara, *Sovereignty and Authenticity. Manchukuo and the East Asian Modern*, Lanham, Rowman & Littlefield Publishers, 2003, p. 60.
[206] See Janis Mimura, *Planning for Empire: Reform Bureaucrats and the Japanese Wartime State*, Ithaca, NY, Cornell University Press, 2011.
[207] Annika A. Culver, *Glorify the Empire. Japanese Avant-Garde Propaganda in Manchukuo*, Vancouver, The University of British Columbia, 2013, p. 140.
[208] *Japanese Techniques of Occupation: Key Laws and Official Documents*, Vol. 2: Manchukuo, Part 1, Washington, DC, Board of Economic Warfare, 1943.

forces. So, although the more important formal political and bureaucratic positions were filled by the Chinese, the number of Japanese both at the national and local level increased significantly, going up to more than fifty percent of the posts at the end of 1930.[209]

As in many other dictatorships of the Era of Fascism, Manchukuo created a single party as well. A party created from above, and avoiding the name "party": the Concordia Association. As a single party, the Concordia Association developed itself as "an arm of the Manchukuo government," becoming a mass party with propaganda departments and an extended network of local and sectorial organizations.[210] The party was progressively modeled around the example of the Japan's IRAA, but with a very important difference: If in Japan the IRAA never controlled the state, in Manchukuo the single party became a central political institution, partially amalgamating with the state. As one of its students wrote, by 1942, "the Concordia Association National Federated Deliberative Assembly had already become one of the major focuses of national policy ... With this degree of amalgamation between government and the Kyowakai, in fact, the Manchukuo Legislative Yuan virtually abdicated its functions entirely to the Assembly."[211] The Assembly was already partially organized in corporatists terms and its guidelines emphasized its role as a "family conference."[212]

With a strong presence of Japanese settlers and other nationalities and ethnic groups, Machukuo was always presented as a country of multiethnic harmony and racial equality.[213] In the 1930s, while debates raged in Japan about the nature of Manchukuo's statehood under Japanese auspices, Japanese officials and members of the Kwantung Army began to create an ideological framework for the new state. Young technocrats from Japan would comprise an important part of this endeavor. These young intellectual-politicians "attempted to bring these same ideals to fruition in the corporatist state of Manchukuo."[214] It is also interesting to note that Manchukuo itself sent missions to Axis Europe. In 1942, for example, a provincial Kyowakai official travelled to Germany and

---

[209] Yamamuro Shin'ichi, *Manchuria under Japanese Dominion*, Philadelphia, University of Pennsylvania Press, 2006, pp. 118–122.
[210] See David George Egler, "Japanese mass organizations in Manchuria, 1928–1945: the ideology of racial harmony," Ph. D. Dissertation, The University of Arizona, 1977, p. vi.
[211] Egler, *Japanese mass organizations in Manchuria, 1928–1945*, p. 312.
[212] Egler, *Japanese mass organizations in Manchuria, 1928–1945*, p. 312.
[213] See Rana Mitter, *The Manchurian Myth Nationalism, Resistance, and Collaboration in Modern China*, Berkeley, The University of California Press, 2000, p. 89.
[214] Culver, *Glorify the Empire*, p. 136.

was "impressed by their mass mobilization organs."[215] In October 1942, a National Patriotic Labor Service law went into effect, for some scholars, "in emulation of the German experience."[216] Social Corporatism was very compatible with the economic project of Manchukuo, which according to Janis Mimura promoted "priority of public interests over the interests of one particular class; comprehensive development of the economy and resources through state control of important industries; encouragement of foreign capital and technology, especially from the advanced countries; and close economic cooperation between Japan and Manchuria."[217] Although the different types of occupation in Asia did not, in many cases, create occupation political regimes, social corporatism became an imperialist institutional tool for the societies under Japanese rule.

Wang Jingwei's "Reorganized National Government of China"

Between 1927 and 1938, against a complex national and international backdrop, Chiang Kai-shek and his allies successfully established an authoritarian political regime in China, which garnered recognition from the international community following their rupture with the communists.[218] With its capital in Nanjing, the nascent Chinese republic, although not exercising control over the entire Chinese territory and consistently beset by conflicts, epitomized the multifaceted challenges inherent in constructing a dictatorship during the Era of Fascism. In 1937, however, the Second Sino-Japanese War began with the Marco Polo Bridge Incident; the Japanese Army occupied the most important and developed parts of China and Chiang Kai-shek returned to the "United Front" between the Kuomintang and the Communists against the Japanese invasion.

Japan created in occupied areas of China several "client" states, namely the Provisional Government of the Republic of China (Zhonghua minguo linshi zhengfu; PGROC) in December 1937 and, in eastern China, the Reformed Government of the Republic of China (Zhonghua minguo weixin zhengfu; RGROC), in 1938.[219] The crucial step toward the creation

---

[215] Egler, Japanese mass organizations in Manchuria, 1928–1945, p. 257.
[216] Ibid.
[217] Mimura, *Planning for Empire*, p. 60.
[218] A good description of its functioning remains Hung-Mao Tien, *Government and Politics in Kuomintang China, 1927–1937*, Stanford, CA, Stanford University Press, 1972. See also Brian Tsui, *China's Conservative Revolution: The Quest for a New Order, 1927–1949*, Cambridge, Cambridge University Press, 2018.
[219] See Margherita Zanasi, "Collaboration, resistance and accommodation in Northeast Asia," in Bosworth and Maiolo, eds., *The Cambridge History of the Second World War*, pp. 509–532.

a new regime under Japanese military occupation, though, would come with the arrival of Wang Jingwei, a dissident and former rival of Chiang Kai-shek in Nanjin, accompanied later by Chen Gongbo, a former minister and member of his faction of the Kuomintang (KMT). Both left Chongqing, the wartime capital of the "National Government" headed by Chiang Kai-shek, and offered collaboration to Japan. Institutional design in Japanese-occupied China took then a decisive turn, and "instead of the confederation of regional governments initially fostered by the occupation armies, Japan's government decided to support the project put forward by former Chinese Premier Wang Jingwei."[220] Wang applied strong pressure for a high level of autonomy, but he was forced to recognize Manchukuo, the separatist regime in northern China, and the presence of the Japanese Army in many areas formally under his control. Last but not least, he was forced to modernize his own army, since Japan was still hoping to settle a peace deal with Chiang Kai-shek at the expenses of his regime.[221]

Considering himself the legitime successor of the Nationalist Republic and accusing Chiang Kai-shek of subservience to the communists, Wang Jingwei, "in sharp contrast with most collaborationist leaders under Axis rule ... did not see collaboration with the occupiers as an opportunity to replace a reviled prewar political regime. On the contrary, he sought to restore the National Government ... which he had led alongside Chiang Kai-shek in the 1930s."[222] As a dissident of Chiang Kai-shek, in 1939 Wang Jingwei and some of his followers organized a "6th Congress" of the KMT criticizing the absence of democracy under Chiang Kai-shek's leadership. But once he established the "Reorganized National Government" (RNG), in 1940, continuity with the single-party-state system was the dominant institutional structure of the new regime.

Wang Jingwei was already the main leader of a faction within Republican China, but the new single party became a bit more unified than the previous one, although it was sometimes forced to make

---

[220] David Serfass, "From constitutional mirage to party hegemony. Building the Wang Jingwei regime in Japanese-occupied China (1939–1942)," in Pinto and Adnolfi, eds., *Building Dictatorships under Axis Rule*, p. 266; and his article, "Collaboration and state making in China: Defining the occupation state, 1937–1945," *Twentieth-Century China*, 47, no. 1 (2022), pp. 71–80.

[221] David P. Barrett, "The Wang Jingwei regime, 1940–45: Continuities and disjunctures with nationalist China," in David P. Barrett and Larry N. Shyu, eds., *Chinese Collaboration with Japan, 1932–1945. The Limits of Accommodation*, Stanford, CA, Stanford University Press, 2001, p. 113.

[222] Serfass, "From constitutional mirage to party hegemony," p. 266.

coalitions as well.²²³ The influence of Prime Minister Konoe Fumimaro's (partly failed) creation of the single party of Authoritarian Japan, the IRAA, in 1940, was also a model for the new KMT of the RNG, legitimizing a "one-party-centered system." As president of the Legislative Yuan, Wang nominated his deputy Chen Gongbo. Regardless of the legitimation of the RNG as the continuation of Republican China and the autonomy in the institution- building of the regime, Japan established "advisors" in every ministry, important legislation had to be submitted to the Japanese Military authorities, and monetary and fiscal policies were defined mostly by these Japanese "advisors."

As in many dictatorships under Axis rule, overall, the regime "had a weak institutional nature" and "exceptional attention was focused on the leader as an integrating force."²²⁴ Some months after the foundation of the regime, the adoption of some of the institutions and political styles of the dictatorships of the Era of Fascism was quite evident in several domains, starting with the leader himself. One year after the creation of RNG, the Ministry of Propaganda started to build a "leadership cult" with fascist overtones, and Wang Jingwei started to be presented in uniform (especially after the declaration of war to the Allies, in January 1943) and his speeches and slogans popularized.²²⁵ In 1942, in a more fascistic replica of the "New Life Movement" of Republican China in the early 1930s, RNG created the New Citizens Movement (NCM), whose "Fundamentals" were written by Wang Jingwei. Under it, "a quasi-military Youth Corps" was created, later combined with other organizations to form a new Youth League. Always associated with an anti-Western imperialism, an ideological element of Japan's expansion in Southeast Asia as well, the "RNG thus came to adopt the language, aesthetics, and many of the accoutrements of the Axis states."²²⁶ Nevertheless, as Jeremy E. Taylor sharply wrote, "It would be a mistake, however, to see the RNG's 'fascist turn' as purely the result of Japanese influence, for fascism was nothing new to Republican China."²²⁷

One strong element of continuity between Nationalist China and the RNG regime is related to the institutionalization of social corporatism, since its main authors coincided in both regimes. The attempt at the

---

[223] Jeremy E. Taylor, *Iconographies of Occupation: Visual Cultures in Wang Jingwei's China, 1939–1945*, Honolulu, University of Hawai'i Press, 2021, p. 20.
[224] Barrett, "The Wang Jingwei regime, 1940–45," p. 104.
[225] See Taylor, *Iconographies of Occupation*, pp. 59–87.
[226] Taylor, *Iconographies of Occupation*, p. 33.
[227] Taylor, *Iconographies of Occupation*, p. 36.

institutionalization of the corporatist framework in Republican China took place during the coalition between Wang Jingwei and Chiang Kai-shek that spanned from January 1932 to December 1935. It was under Wang's leadership that this effort was undertaken, with decisive interventions from Industry Minister Chen Gongbo, who was also a member of the Wang faction.[228] This segment of the nationalist elite had the most well-defined vision for the construction of an economically and politically unified China within a centralized state, capable of reacting to the 1929 crisis and the Japanese threat with an autarchic developmental model. In contrast to Chiang Kai-shek's approach, which was more oriented toward military needs, this group's strategy focused on developing a more national and nationalist "Minzu" economy "as the only effective means of nation building."[229] As its best student noted, this group seems to "have been particularly attracted by the Italian Fascist model of nation building and economic modernity." Like many other fascist-era dictatorships, they selectively incorporated elements from this model, choosing "the aspects that resonated most with their political vision and with China's own circumstances."[230]

Once leaders of the RNG, Wang Jingwei and Chen Gongbo reorganized and adapted its main economic and social institutions to the new regime. They established a new National Economic Council (NEC), that "was supposed to create the same structure of economic control established by its predecessor in the 1930s. Like the 1930s NEC, the new one aimed at bringing the Chinese economy under the control of the Chinese government and away from the Japanese."[231] For obvious reasons there was some opposition from the occupying authorities. The corporatism labor legislation of the RNG was in strong continuity with nationalist China. In continuity with nationalist China as well were the references to Italian corporatism: "Laudatory references to Italy continued under the Wang Jingwei regime and popularized the myth that fascist corporatism constituted an alternative to capitalism and socialism. The NRG's Ministry of Social Affairs published articles in its bulletin outlining Italy's social-welfare legislation."[232]

---

[228] See the groundbreaking study by Margherita Zanasi, *Saving the Nation: Economic Modernity in Republican China*, Chicago, IL, University of Chicago Press, 2006.

[229] Zanasi, *Saving the Nation*, p. 3. On Chen Gongbo's Corporatist projects, see also Margherita Zanasi, "Chen Gongbo and the construction of a modern nation in 1930s China," in Timothy Brook and Andre Schmid, eds., *Nation Work: Asian Elites and National Identities*, Ann Arbor, University of Michigan Press, 2000, pp. 125–157.

[230] Zanasi, *Saving the Nation*, pp. 12 and 14.

[231] Zanasi, *Saving the Nation*, p. 216.

[232] Joshua H. Howard, "Beyond repression and resistance: Worker agency and corporatism in occupied Nanjing," *Modern Asian Studies*, 56, no. 1 (2022), p. 21.

Burma under Ba Maw: "One Blood, One Voice, One Leader"

When Japan invaded Burma with the support of Thailand in December 1941, as in the case of the Philippines under US rule, there was already a "self-government." After the separation of Burma from British India in 1937, the colonial power established a Constitution and allowed the creation of political parties and elections to a parliament; other representative institutions were in the making.[233] During the initial months of the war, the British strategy in political terms was to maintain its colonial government ruling with emergency powers until the reinstatement of the 1937 Constitution and the reestablishment of a government based on it.[234]

With the occupation of Burma, the standard procedure of establishing a Japanese Military Administration (JMA) was followed. This JMA was subordinate to the Southern Area Army, directed from Singapore, and was autonomous from the Imperial Army. Like other Japanese military administrations, it had a large number of civilian officials in its service and, as in Europe occupied by Nazi Germany, had "rival centres of authority" and "divergent points of view ... among the Japanese themselves (especially civilians versus Army officers)."[235] This tension continued after formal independence, giving the government some room for maneuver. On the other hand, the British colonial administrative structure was essentially maintained, as were most of its officials.

Under the JMA, a native government structure was created almost immediately, which changed its name until formal independence in August 1943. But the JMA kept the legislative power in its hands, placed "advisors" in the government with veto power, and restricted its territorial powers, keeping control of the frontier, with many economic resources and infrastructures, under Japanese direct administration.[236] This Burmese "Executive Administration," and the "Burma Preparatory Commission for Independence" designed the political institutions of the new regime and had prominent nationalists in its service, the most prominent being Ba Maw and Aung Sang. From there to independence the steps were rapid, and under the leadership of Ba Maw and the decisive role of the JMA, this

---

[233] Paul H. Kratoska and Ken'ichi Goto, "Japanese occupation of Southeast Asia, 1941–1945," in Bosworth and Maiolo, eds., *The Cambridge History of the Second World War*, p. 539.
[234] Robert H. Taylor, *The State in Burma*, Honolulu, University of Hawaii Press, 1987, p. 224.
[235] Donald M. Seekins, *Burma and Japan since 1940. From "Co-prosperity" to "Quiet Dialogue,"* Copenhagen, NIAS — Nordic Institute of Asian Studies, 2007, p. 16.
[236] Trager, ed., *Burma. Japanese Military Administration. Selected Documents, 1941–1945*, pp. 120–121.

"Preparatory Commission for Independence," made up of politicians and leaders of the main interest associations, discussed and approved in three months the relevant legislation for independence. The Commission then dissolved, but its members were retained as a State Assembly that proclaimed independence.

Ba Maw was already a prominent veteran nationalist politician, for many even "arguably pre-war Burma's foremost political leader," when Burma was occupied.[237] With a cosmopolitan academic background, his political career under British rule in the 1930s included being Education Minister and then Prime Minister in 1937, already under the new Constitution. With his government overthrown in 1939, Ba Maw and his party opposed any participation in the war on the side of the UK, especially since Churchill called on Burmese nationalists to enter the war while refusing to offer any conditions for independence in return (and even repressing them). Ba Maw would end up in prison and was preparing to be tried when he escaped, initiated contact with the Japanese, and ended up being the head of the government during the entire period of the Japanese occupation.[238] Another Burmese who (although with a different path from Ba Maw) became a very important leader under occupation was Aung Sang, another nationalist activist, who became a member of the Communist party for a short period, fled to China, and began collaboration with Japan. Clandestinely reentering Burma with a "Burma Independence Army" (BIA), Aung Sang fought with the Japanese Armed Forces during the invasion. After some hesitation though, the Japanese administration ended up choosing Ba Maw as head of the collaborationist political structure, placing Aung Sang as the second figure (Minister of Defense), responsible for the reorganization of the BIA, which became the Japanese-trained "Burma Defense Army" (BDA) after the occupation. Some of its cadres would be sent to military academies in Japan and, under the supervision of the Japanese Army, participated in the war alongside it.

The dissolution of the existing parties under British rule and the creation of a single party was quickly decided (still under the JMA), and Ba Maw then founded the Dobama Sinyetha Asi Ayon (Poor Man's Party, also known as the National Service Association). The new single party was a party built from above and based on the forced unification of two parties.

---

[237] Michael W. Charney, *A History of Modern Burma*, Cambridge, Cambridge University Press, 2009, p. 56.
[238] Taylor, *The State in Burma*, pp. 171–172.

It was reorganized after independence by Ba Maw under the name Greater Burma Party, and given even more power and unity in the construction of the "New Order." After independence, membership in the party of civil servants became mandatory. On the nature of the new single party, it is worth quoting Ba Maw's own words in his memoirs written many years later, recalling that, "In accordance with our political belief at the time, the power structure of the party was a dictatorship based upon the leadership principle of 'One blood, One voice, One leader.' Like the other Axis nations – and in fact even some of their enemies had also gone totalitarian, to fight totalitarianism, as they very carefully explained – the Japanese believed in the leadership principle and would only deal with us on that basis."[239] Maw also did not forget to point out that the development of the single party "was the beginning of total mobilization" and that "the task was completed by following it up with functional associations."[240]

In January 1943, Prime Minister Tojo announced the project of independence of Burma and the Philippines in the Japanese Diet. As in other projects for the establishment of autonomous political regimes, the Japanese authorities had very clear guidelines for the establishment of a dictatorship. The "Guiding Principles for the Independence of Burma" pointed toward the creation of a single party from above, with a dictator as head of the new state, stating that "in the event that a Parliament is created, attention must be paid to prevent the Parliament from interfering with the Head of State and his execution of the affairs of state," preferring an advisory chamber, and suggesting that a "House of Councilors (a tentative name) ... [be] established as an advisory body."[241] These guiding principles shaped the interim Constitution of 1943, according to which Burma was now led by a "Head of State," who in fact had the functions and powers of Prime Minister, and the new state would become "co-equal member of the community of sovereign states forming the Greater East Asia Co-Prosperity sphere."[242] A Privy Council was created with advisory functions to the Head of State and its members were appointed by him. Legislative powers belonged to the Head of State, and "All appointments in the services of the State [were to be] derived from the

---

[239] Ba Maw, *Breakthrough in Burma: Memoirs of a Revolution, 1939–1946*, New Haven, CT, Yale University Press, 1968, p. 280. See also Ba Maw cited in Trager, ed., *Burma. Japanese Military Administration. Selected Documents, 1941–1945*, p. 174.
[240] Maw, *Breakthrough in Burma*, p. 280.
[241] Trager, ed., *Burma. Japanese Military Administration. Selected Documents, 1941–1945*, p. 145.
[242] Trager, ed., *Burma. Japanese Military Administration*, p. 158.

Head of the State" as well. The description of the formal concentration of power in the figure of the "Head of State" could continue, because until the creation of a "Constituent Body ... truly representative of the Burmese people and of its opinion," but appointed by the Head of State, the latter's power was formally total.[243]

With the declaration of independence, Ba Maw became the "Naingandaw Adipadi" (Head of State), although for many observers of the time, "Adipadi" was "the nearest Burmese equivalent to 'duce' or 'Führer'."[244] The authoritarian nationalist slogans repeated by Ba Maw and by the single party (such as the already-mentioned "One Voice, One Blood, One Nation") clearly followed the trends of the Era of Fascism "in German, Italian, and Japanese politics throughout the 1930s and 1940s," responding to the debate in the Burmese press on "the question of who would be Burma's Mussolini or Hitler" as leader of an ultranationalist version of nation-state building.[245] However, even though the provisional constitution gave him almost equivalent total powers, Japanese control over Ba Maw and his regime was nevertheless huge. The "New State" of Ba Maw was obviously controlled by a Japanese shadow structure, similar to the one present in most of the "independent states" under Axis rule. In the case of Burma, this was achieved through Japanese advisors in each Ministry and with Gotaro Ogawa as "Supreme Advisor to the Burmese Government."[246] Ogawa was a conservative civilian politician, university professor, financial expert, and former minister of trade and industry of Japan.[247] A secret military agreement with Japan was signed as well.

In his proclamation of independence on August 1, 1943, declaring war on the Allies on the same day ("the present Great East Asiatic War is Burma's war"), Ba Maw associated Japan with liberation from Western colonialism, and the creation of the "New State" of Burma with its integration into the Greater East Asia Co-Prosperity Sphere.[248] In Burma's "New Order Plan," signed by Ba Maw, he described the political project of the "New State." In addition to the consolidation of the government, the

---

[243] Trager, ed., *Burma. Japanese Military Administration*, p. 163.
[244] Geoffrey Sawer, "The return of the puppets in South-East Asia," *Australian Outlook*, 1947, p. 8.
[245] Taylor, *The State in Burma*, p. 284.
[246] Seekings, *Burma and Japan since 1940*, p. 220.
[247] Michael W. Charney and Atsuko Naono, "The Burmese Economy under the Japanese Occupation, 1942–1945," in Marcel Boldorf and Tetsuji Okazaki, eds., *Economies under Occupation. The Hegemony of Nazi Germany and Imperial Japan in World War II*, London, Routledge, 2015, p. 220.
[248] See Trager, ed., *Burma. Japanese Military Administration*, p. 168.

state apparatus, the armed forces, and the single party, under its leadership, the organizational frame of society was defined in detail. Following the model that Japan implemented in directly administered territories, and considering it "a Burmese version of the New Life Movement," the plan provided for the creation of an extensive organizational network and corporatist structures, with youth associations, interest organizations, and a "Labor Organization," covering "the population from top to bottom." In the words of Ba Maw, "the whole structure will be kept together by the principle of Burmese unity in one blood, one voice, one leader which has been affirmed in our Declaration of Independence."[249]

Ba Maw's "one-party pseudo-fascist state" lasted two years.[250] In mid 1944, Japanese Minister Tojo decorated Ba Maw and Aung San but a year later, with the turn of the war against Tokyo, parts of the BNA itself rebelled against the Japanese military and Aung Sang initiated contacts with the British and the Burmese opposition. Ba Maw and other members of his government accompanied the Japanese withdrawal, imprisoned alongside the Japanese elite after the Allied occupation.

The Philippines under Laurel: "One Party, One People, One President, One Government"

Japanese Armed Forces invaded the Philippines a few hours after the attack on Pearl Harbor, but did not reach Manila until January of the following year. Although the majority of the local elite immediately began collaborating with the Japanese invader, President Manuel L. Quezon formed a government-in-exile in the USA, as the Philippines was in the midst of a transition to independence (scheduled for 1946) and his government was already vested with great autonomy by a Filipino political elite.

After the establishment of a Japanese Military Administration (JMA), Tojo began, not without some military resistance, plans for the construction of a formally independent state with a dictatorial regime under the strict dependence of the occupier. The JMA immediately set up a "Philippine Executive Commission" (PEC) as a transitional governing institution, with several politicians from the previous period, which was considered a success. The most prominent of these was Jorge B. Vargas, initially chosen by the Japanese military to head the PEC, soon after followed by José P. Laurel. At the time of the invasion, Vargas was the

---

[249] See "Burma's new order plan," in Trager, ed., *Burma. Japanese Military Administration*, pp. 174 and 182.
[250] Taylor, *The State in Burma*, p. 231.

mayor of Manila and already had an extensive political career, having been the executive secretary of President Quezon. Laurel, who offered more confidence to the new occupying administration, also had an extensive career in politics and the judicial system. An admirer of Authoritarian Japan, Laurel didn't come from a radical right-wing political culture either, although his public statements expressed a "debt of honour to the August Virtue of His Majesty, the Emperor of Nippon, for ordaining the holy war and hastening the day of our national deliverance."[251] In various writings and statements before the Japanese invasion, Laurel, although always in the nationalist and independence camp, supported Quezon's "State of Emergency," because he felt that "constitutional dictatorship" was in keeping with a worldwide trend in which "totalitarianism [was] gradually supplanting democracy."[252]

In the Philippines, the creation of the single party preceded the creation of the collaborationist regime, and was an initiative of the Japanese military administration and its Director-General General Takeji, explicitly following the model of the Japanese IRAA and Manchukuo's Concordia Association. It was this military administration that addressed the heads of the parties, announcing their dissolution and the creation of the new single party, the Association for Service to the New Philippines (Kapisanan sa Paglilingkod sa Bagong Pilipinas; KALIBAPI). The executive order for its creation outlined its program objectives: to unify Filipinos from all social classes and promote their social, cultural, and economic well-being and, of course, to integrate Filipinos into the Great East Asia Co-Prosperity Sphere. Led by the head of the PEC, the organizational structure of the party also followed that of the IRAA. Vargas first, and then Laurel, were its leaders (although Benigno Aquino, its Executive Director, had a decisive role in the organization). The party also created a youth organization, the Junior KALIBAPI.[253] The interpenetration between the administration and the organization of KALIBAPI was great, under the motto "one party, one people, one president, one government."[254] Like other

---

[251] Cited in Jonathan Black, "Jose P. Laurel and Jorge B. Vargas: Issues of collaboration and loyalty during the Japanese occupation of the Philippines" (2010). CMC Senior Theses. Paper 69, p. 18.

[252] Cited in David Joel Steinberg, *Philippine Collaboration in World War II*, Ann Arbor, The University of Michigan Press, 1967, p. 77.

[253] Steinberg, *Philippine Collaboration in World War II*, p. 62.

[254] Cited in Ricardo T. Jose, "The Association for Service to the New Philippines (KALIGAPI) during the Japanese occupation: Attempting to transplant a Japanese wartime concept to the Philippines," *The Journal of Sophia Asian Studies*, 19 (2001), p. 171. For a very detailed analysis of its activity, see pp. 149–185.

single parties of the time, KALIBAPI was created from above and tried to force from above the unification of the leaders of parties that had since been dissolved. Its program was of Pan-Asian anti-Western nationalism allied to Japan, and it was marked by Japanese intellectual-politicians such as Royama Masamichi and the Showa Research Association, the main radical-right think tank of Japanese Prime Minister Prince Konoe.[255] The party played a central role in the institutional engineering of "Independence" in 1943, legitimizing the approval of the new Constitution and occupying as a single party the previously elective seats in the new National Assembly. Undergoing an adaptation to the new political institutions, with independence the fundamental structure was maintained.

In June 1943, the liaison conference of Japan approved the "Outline for the Guiding of Philippine Independence," accelerating the transition to the formation of the regime. The collaborationist elite had considerable leeway to create the institutions of the Second Philippine Republic; with the creation of the "Preparatory Commission for Philippine Independence" (PCPI), the process developed rapidly. As in many other cases of occupation regimes, Japan carried out and forced the signing of a secret agreement in which the new state was obliged to provide Japan with control of enormous economic resources, from mines to factories important for war industries, air transportation, ports, and allowed for the military occupation of the territory and participation in the War "at the appropriate moment."[256]

Laurel and the twenty members of PCPI discussed and approved the new constitution in September 1943. The new authoritarian constitution reformed that of the more liberal Commonwealth Constitution of 1935, moving it into an authoritarian direction: it diminished the legislative powers of the National Assembly, making the presidency the locus of power with great autonomy from the Assembly; the election of the president became indirect; governors were appointed by the President; the 1935 Constitution's "Declaration of Human Rights" was changed to become the "Duties and Rights of the Citizen" and the Judiciary was weakened as well.[257] The Supreme Court, for example, could only declare laws

---

[255] See Sven Matthienssen, *Japanese Pan-Asianism and the Philippines from the Late 19th Century to the End of World War II: Going to the Philippines Is Like Coming Home?*, Leiden, Brill, 2016, pp. 132–139, and Sven Matthiessen, "Re-orienting the Philippines: The KALIBAPI party and the application of Japanese Pan-Asianism, 1942–45," *Modern Asian Studies* 53, no. 2 (2019), pp. 560–581.

[256] Yellen, *The Greater East Asia Co-Prosperity Sphere*, p. 184.

[257] The Constitution of 1943, Official Gazette, www.officialgazette.gov.ph/constitutions/the-1943-constitution/, retrieved December 27, 2024.

unconstitutional through a unanimous vote, where in 1935, it could do so with two-thirds of the votes.

A unicameral National Assembly would be constituted, in theory, by some "functional" MPs and some elected: Forty-six provincial governors and eight mayors of chartered cities were automatically appointed to this chamber. Another fifty-four were chosen by the local organization of the single party, KALIBAPI, but, in reality, they were selected from above.[258] Despite being scrutinized on the basis of political obedience, many MPs already came from the commonwealth period.

As the main newspaper of the Philippines wrote in an editorial, the new "one-party regime" was "peaceful, inexpensive, [and] efficient."[259] Acknowledging the dependent nature of the new collaborationist regime, whose "independence" still provoked some dissension among the military elite, the Director-General of the JMA, General Takaji Wachi, thus defined Japan's role: "Japan will hold the position of a protector ... but the Philippines will not be a protectorate."[260] Needless to say that the Japanese East Asia Ministry filed a plan "urging the appointment of Japanese 'consultants' to every agency of the Philippine government."[261]

With José P. Laurel as president, this short lived "Second Philippine Republic," was inaugurated in October 1943 before a court of Japanese dignitaries and 500,000 Filipinos, and was immediately recognized by Japan, its Axis allies, and partners of the "Co-Prosperity Sphere," namely, Germany, Italy, Bulgaria, Croatia, and Hungary, as well as Thailand, Burma, Manchukuo, Wang Jingwei's RNG, and Francoist Spain (conditionally).[262] Laurel's "Second Philippine Republic" lasted less than two years but its end would be identical to several others under Japanese military occupation, or the European poles of the Axis, with its government evacuated to Baguio in December 1944, and later to Tokyo, in March 1945.

5 Making States and Regimes under Axis Rule: Concluding Remarks

The expansion of Axis rule in Europe and East Asia during World War II was responsible for an impressive growth of authoritarian "occupation" regimes. Starting in Asia with the imperialist expansion of Japan, followed by a more modest expansion of Fascist Italy in Africa and in the

---

[258] Steinberg, *Philippine Collaboration in World War II*, pp. 82–83.
[259] Cited in Steinberg, *Philippine Collaboration in World War II*, p. 83.
[260] Cited in Steinberg, *Philippine Collaboration in World War II*, p. 82
[261] See Steinberg, *Philippine Collaboration in World War II*, p. 82.
[262] See Steinberg, *Philippine Collaboration in World War II*, p. 85.

Balkans, and that of Germany in Europe, the number of dictatorships increased substantially. From this perspective, 1942 may have represented the apex of the global wave of autocratization associated with the Era of Fascism, when "the Axis empires seemed to be very close indeed to the realization of their new imperial world order."[263] Its dominant poles (Nazi Germany, Fascist Italy and Authoritarian Japan) constituted then the most decisive centers of political diffusion and coercive transfers to authoritarian elites, parties, and political regimes. Following territorial expansion and the development of the war, new dictatorships, hybrid authoritarian political institutions, and occupation administrations were imposed or conditioned by the occupier. When they did not create formally autonomous or independent states, the various types of administration of the military-occupied territories also suffered the imposition of political, social, and economic institutions that already marked the political systems of their poles. Regardless of the diversity of occupation regimes, from annexation, to military administrations, protectorates, Reichskommissariat, or formal "independent states," there was a clear wave of creation and reorganization of political and social institutions based in Italian Fascism and German National Socialism, with the presence of "third way" authoritarian projects associated with the radical right as well.[264] Overall, the dynamics of global institutional diffusion – especially of Italian Fascism, already dominantly present in the 1930s – was followed by that of the coercive transfers of authoritarian institutions by the Axis powers on the territories and countries under their military control. This dynamic of diffusion and coercive transfers was always controlled, with rare exceptions, by the "advisors" of the occupying force with veto power (who were in each administration), which made the institutional diversity more significant.

Military administration was, as Philipe Morgan has pointed out, "the default position" desired by many segments of the Axis armed forces during World War II, but Hitler's initial promise quickly faded.[265] This option turned out to be minoritarian in Europe, and more adopted in Asia by Authoritarian Japan, although in several cases only as transitory, occurring in the wake of formally independent regimes. The explanation for this difference, however, does not pertain only to the obvious centrality of the armed forces in the war and in the control of the occupied territories,

---

[263] Hedinger and von Brescius, "The German and Japanese empires. Great power competition and the world wars in trans-Imperial perspective," p. 1149.
[264] See Pinto, ed., *An Authoritarian Third Way in the Era of Fascism*.
[265] Morgan, *Hitler's Collaborators*, p. 43.

but to the fact that the armed forces, although with internal tensions, were much more important in the political system of the Japanese dictatorship than in National Socialism or in the Italian fascist regime.

Although there were many Nazi plans and projects for a more coherent European "New Order," the "polyocratic" character of its political system and of the decision-making process, which was extended to the occupied territories, made it difficult to recognize coherence "amidst this polyphony."[266] This characteristic of National Socialism occupation policies has even led some scholars such as Ian T. Gross to propose that it was "neither possible nor fruitful to devise a systematic conceptual framework and typology for the study of regimes of occupation in Europe."[267] We can nevertheless to briefly draw some de facto dominant strategic options of the three poles of the Axis in terms of political administration and coercive transfers of authoritarian institutions to occupied territories and countries.

Although it was the weakest military power in the Axis, the projects of Italian Fascism in the Balkans, both in Albania and in other occupied territories, were marked by the export of their political institutions, with special emphasis on the single party and the corporatist institutions. Although in some cases the autonomy of some "Independent States" was significant, and the dependence shared with Germany was important, as in the case of Croatia, the Italian model was the dominant one. As we have already seen, even if the coercive transfer of Italian fascist institutions was limited, its diffusion in Axis Europe exceeded by far its territorial domination. In Serbia, for example, German occupation authorities refused local projects to build a regime they associated with the influence of fascist Italy, and in Croatia, Pavelić tried to conciliate the institutions of his regime under the discreet pressure of Nazi Germany. Other examples were present in military-occupied Europe.

The Reichskommissariat type of political administration of occupied territories seems to have been the dominant model for Nazi Germany. Led by senior members of the Nazi elite nominated and answering directly to Hitler, these Reichskommissariate ran from purged and controlled native administrations, as in the case of the Netherlands or Norway, to those closer to a limited "self-government" in the case of the Baltic States, suffering interference and tensions with parallel structures, ranging from the military elite to the NASDP, the SS, and sometimes from the Reich ministries themselves. In 1941, the creation of the Ministry for the Occupied Eastern Territories

---

[266] Bauer, *The Construction of a National Socialist Europe during the Second World War*, p. 3.
[267] Gross, *Polish Society under German Occupation*, p. 32.

under Alfred Rosenberg (which would administer the territories newly conquered from the Soviet Union) did not change the pattern described.

Rarer were military administrations controlling secretaries-general of dependent native ministries or "self-governments," as in the cases of Belgium and Serbia. The Protectorate of Bohemia and Moravia had specific aspects, such as having a Reichsprotektor with theoretically more limited functions, and a native and formally autonomous government with authoritarian political institutions.

Regardless of the type of direct administration, the Nazi authorities created or pragmatically accepted the reorganization of social corporatist institutions but tended to reject the offer of native radical right elites and parties to create and eventually govern under its rule. The cases of Belgium and Netherlands are particularly illustrative. In Belgium, they rejected the project, associated with the king, to create an authoritarian regime and a single party from above, the "Parti des Provinces Romanes." In the Netherlands, after some hesitations, the NU was dissolved by Reichskommissar Seyss-Inquart. Ambitions of local fascists to come to power were also refused in Belgium and the Netherlands, although in Norway they gave Quisling the opportunity to try to build a regime for a short period of time (Table 3; Table 4) The ambitions of many of these fascist parties were also played out in the "polyocratic" corridors of Nazi Germany.

When we look at other parts of Europe, it seems empirically accurate to note that in most cases, the response from Nazi Germany to the pressure "from below" by a plurality of collaborationist elites was not consistent, sometimes opting for different combinations among them. Nevertheless, at party level, German rule had an important consequence: the autonomous survival, and sometimes even the development, of national fascist parties in situations where the authoritarian elites dominated institution-building, limiting the capacity of the authoritarian collaborationist elites to build a single party from above and penetrating collaborationist administrations (Table 3).

Mostly minor political movements in the 1930s, the small fascist parties became important in Axis Europe. Although they saw their access to power denied or conditioned in most cases, from France, to Belgium or the Netherlands, they were the most loyal parties dedicated to the service of the occupier, fulfilling functions of threatening authoritarian alternatives to governments and institutions of collaboration, providing cadres to the occupation administrations, and also of political and ideological mobilization and paramilitary volunteers in the service of Nazi Germany. From the Waffen SS

Table 3 Parties and Party Systems under Axis Rule in Europe

Dominant power	Country or region	Period	Parties	Party system	Ideology
Italy	Albania	1939–43	Albanian Fascist Party	Single	Fascist
Germany	Belgium	1940	Parti des Provinces Romanes (failed)	No	Radical Right
		1940–45	Rexist Party		Fascist
		1940–45	Flemish National League		Fascist
Germany	Bohemia and Moravia	1939–45	National Partnership	Dominant	Radical Right
		1939–45	National Fascist Community		Fascist
Italy-Germany	Croatia	1941–45	Ustasha	Single	Fascist
Germany	Denmark	1940–45	Several National Socialist Labour Party (DNSAP)	Multi-party	–
					Fascist
Germany	Estonia	–	None	No	–
Germany	France	1940–45	French Popular Party (PPF)	No	Fascist
			Franciste Movement		Fascist
			National Popular Rally (RPN)		Fascist
Germany	Greece	1941–44	National Socialist Union of Greece	No	Fascist
			Greek National Socialist Party		Fascist
Germany	Hungary	1940–44	Party of National Unity	Dominant	Radical Right
		1944–45	Arrow Cross Party	Single	Fascist
Germany	Italy (RSI)	1943–45	Republican Fascist Party (PFR)	Single	Fascist

(*Continued*)

Table 3 (Continued)

Dominant power	Country or region	Period	Parties	Party system	Ideology
Germany	Latvia	–	None	No	–
Germany	Lithuania	–	None	No	–
Germany	Netherlands	1940–45	Netherlands Union (1940–41, dissolved) National Socialist Movement in the Netherlands (NSB)	No	Radical Right Fascist
Germany	Norway	1940–45	National Unity	Single	Fascist
Germany	Serbia	1941–44	United Militant Labour Organization (ZBOR)	No	Fascist
Germany	Slovakia	1939–45	Slovak People's Party	Single	Fascist

Source: Created by the author.

Table 4 Parties and Party Systems under Axis Rule in Asia

Dominant power	Country or region	Period	Parties	Party system	Ideology
Japan	Burma	1942–45	Greater Burma Party	Single	Radical Right (Nationalist)
Japan	Manchukuo	1932–45	Concordia Association	Single	Radical Right (Nationalist)
Japan	Reorganized National Government of the Republic of China	1940–45	New Kuomintang	Single	Radical Right (Nationalist)
Japan	Java	1942–43	Centre of the People's Power (PUTERA)	Single	Radical Right (Nationalist)
		1944	Java Service Association (1944)	Single	Radical Right (Nationalist)
Japan	Philippines	1942–45	KALIBAPI	Single	Radical Right (Nationalist)
Japan	Thailand	1941–45	People's Party	Dominant	Radical Right (Nationalist)

Source: Created by the author.

to the auxiliary militia battalions of the repression and deportation of Jewish and other segments of societies under occupation, they were the most loyal agents of the occupying power and of legitimation of last resort, of which the constitution of the "Government of National Unity" of the Hungarian Arrow Cross in 1944 is an example. This dimension of collaboration is almost entirely absent in East Asia under Japanese rule, either simply because there were no fascist parties, or because their "functional equivalents" were less used by the occupier's administrations. Here, if radicalization was also present, there were other agents of collaboration, mainly nationalist.

There are different reasons to explain why formal "Independent States," like Vichy or the Slovak State were maintained, but unlike in the case of Japan, there is not a coherent strategy to create them, even when the pressure from collaborationist nationalist elites, was very much present, like in the Baltic countries. Nazi Germany accepted the creation of the "Slovak State" and formal independence, even if suspicious of its Dollfuss's "clerico-fascist" matrix, and later with its institutions progressively tempered by the spread of Nazi social corporatism. In the case of Vichy's "French State," the institutional constraint on the part of Nazi Germany was not great. The same could be said of other native dictatorships that joined the Axis and came under German dependence, such as Horthy's Hungary or Antonescu's Romania; the latter even authorized eliminating the Iron Guard.

What was sometimes at stake in these institution-building processes was the tension between the radical right and fascists, and often its "forced unification," in these regimes. With the "window of opportunity" of the simultaneous breakdown of democratic regimes and direct or indirect military occupation, different political families took part in authoritarian regime building; however, this should not be interpreted as a global option for authoritarian versus fascist elites or vice versa, and we should be cautious about making generalizations. If in Slovakia the German embassy suspected the construction of "a corporatist system ... in the same spirit as the corporatist system of Dollfuss,"[268] in Norway, the main factor beyond the forced postponement of Quisling's proposals was the resistance of local organized interests and the fear of disruption in the economy of war. It would be a little excessive to say the "Nazi regime exported the organized chaos of its system of rule in Germany to the *tabula rasa* of occupied territories."[269] However, it certainly had "a patchwork character."[270]

---

[268] Hallon, and Schvarc, "Ideas, reality and the international context of the social state in the Slovak Republic of 1939–45," pp. 915–916.
[269] Morgan, *Hitler's Collaborators*, pp.78–79.
[270] G. Wright, *The Ordeal of Total War, 1939–45*, New York, Harper and Row, 1968, p. 29.

After this brief tour of some experiments of political regime institutionalization in Axis Europe, the most salient characteristics of the processes of institution-building presented below is the attempt to institutionalize social and political corporatism. Whether by external imposition – as in the Italian occupation of Albania and Dalmatia – or by national elites – as in the case of German occupations – the different versions of authoritarian corporatism that were proposed by fascists and radical-right elites seem to be the institutional cement of regime-building. From Vichy's constitutional projects to the French Labor Charter, from Quisling's projected corporatist parliament to the constitution of Slovakia, or even Nedić's rejected projects in Serbia, what was at stake in most of these dictatorships were different versions of authoritarian corporatist-based political systems. Social corporatist institutions were introduced in almost all occupied territories in Europe, regardless of the type of administration, and Nazi Germany tended to impose coercive transfers in areas under direct administration and pressure for its own model in formal independent countries, like Slovakia (Table 5). The war and the economy of war was, of course, always the priority, which might explain the block of Quisling's reforms or of the attempt to implement them against the entrepreneurs in the "Italian Social Republic."

Compared to Nazi Germany, Authoritarian Japan had a more coherent strategy for the political control and administration of military occupied territories. Even if different in ideological and political content, the Japanese imperialist project was closer to that of Italian Fascism in terms of coercive transfers of political institutions.[271] In fact, although "military superiority within the occupation regimes was paramount," in terms of social institutions, parties, and ideological legitimation, Japanese administrations, both military and in formal independent States, imposed coercive transfers of institutions being established in Authoritarian Japan itself.[272] On the other hand, although developed in a very large area of East and Southeast Asia, with very diverse political cultures, from China to Java or Thailand, the construction of new states was also more coherent, with the participation of what some historians has defined as "patriotic collaborators" or "collaborationist nationalism," less present in regimes under Axis rule in Europe.[273]

---

[271] For a comparison between foreign policy decision-making in Fascist Italy and Authoritarian Japan, see Ken Ishida, *Japan, Italy and the Road to the Tripartite Alliance*, London, Palgrave, 2019.

[272] Peter M. R. Stirk, *The Politics of Military Occupation*, Edinburgh, Edinburgh University Press, 2009, p. 79.

[273] Yellen, *The Greater East Asia Co-Prosperity Sphere*, p. 20. See Timothy Brook, *Collaboration. Japanese Agents and Local Elites in Wartime China*, Cambridge, MA, Harvard University Press, 2005.

Table 5 Political and Social Corporatism under Axis Rule in Europe

Dominant power	Country or region	Period	Occupation regime	Political corporatism	Social corporatism
Italy	Albania	1939–43	Kingdom of Albania in personal union with Italy (Protectorate)	Yes	Yes
Germany	Belgium	1940–44	Military Administration	No	Yes
Germany		1944–45	Reichskommissariat	No	Yes
Germany	Bohemia and Moravia	1939–45	Protectorate	Yes	Yes
Italy-Germany	Croatia	1941–45	Independent State ("Independent State of Croatia")	Yes	Yes
Germany	Denmark	1940–45	Independent State	No	No
Germany	Estonia	1941–44	Reichskommissariat	No	No
Germany	France	1940–45	Independent State (The "French State")	No	Yes
Italy-Germany	Greece	1941–44	Military Administration	No	No
Germany	Hungary	1940–44	Independent State	No	Yes
Germany		1944–45	Independent State ("Government of National Union")	Yes	Yes
Germany	Italy	1943–45	Independent State ("Italian Social Republic")	Yes	Yes

Germany	Latvia	1941–44	Reichskommissariat	No	No
Germany	Lithuania	1941–45	Reichskommissariat	No	No
Germany	Netherlands	1940–45	Reichskommissariat	No	Yes
Germany	Norway	1940–45	Reichskommissariat	Yes	Yes
Germany	Serbia	1941–44	Military Administration	No	Yes
Germany	Slovakia	1939–45	Independent State ("Slovak State")	Yes	Yes

Source: Created by the author.

In fact, in East Asia, the collaborationist elite was fundamentally nationalist, and the adoption of authoritarian institutions from the Era of Fascism represented not only the forced transposition by the occupier of authoritarian institutions, such as the single party or corporatist institutions, but also a coincidence of perception that these models were associated with what was seen at the time as tools of economic, social, and political modernization in the construction of a post-colonial state.

In 1942, preparing the creation of these new "independent states," Japan created a Ministry of Greater East Asia, replacing the Ministry of Colonial Affairs, to coordinate the development of the "Greater East Asia Co-Prosperity Sphere." In 1943, Japan organized the first and only summit of its "independent" collaborationist dictatorships, the Greater East Asia Conference, where, in addition to Thailand, only regimes recognized by the Axis participated, such as Manchukuo, Wang Jingwei's RNG, Burma, Philippines and also, as an observer, Chandra Bose, as head of "Provisional Government of Free India." Laurel represented the Philippines and Ba Maw represented the "State of Burma." In his address to the Conference, Ba Maw was perhaps the clearest spokesperson for Japanese aspirations when he pointed out that they were "at the same time nationals of their own country and nationals of Greater East Asia."[274] As Ba Maw recalled many years later, "in that Assembly held in Tokyo on November 5 and 6, 1943, the dream of a few Asian dreamers became a reality for millions of people in Asia."[275]

Similar to some (only sketched) plans in Axis Europe, Japan also created some transnational organizations associated with the "Greater Asia Co-Prosperity Sphere," but here much better designed, with conferences and training/mobility programs like the Association of Greater East Asia Journalists, the Greater East Asia Literary Conference, the Greater East Asia People's Conference, the Greater East Asia Medical Conference, and others.

As we saw earlier, the creation of some single parties, from the Philippines to Java, were clearly inspired by the Japanese IRAA, but perhaps the most coherent and transversally imposed political and social project associated with Japan's imperialist expansion was the creation of structures that were transposed across various types of Japanese public administration in Asia and became a general policy (Table 6). Despite the diversity and greater or

---

[274] Cited in kratoska and ken'ichi goto, "Japanese occupation of Southeast Asia, 1941–1945," p. 542.
[275] Maw, *Breakthrough in Burma*, p. 437.

Table 6 Political and Social Corporatism under Axis Rule in Asia

Dominant Power	Country or Region	Period	Occupation Regime	Political Corporatism	Social Corporatism
Japan	Burma	1942–43	Military Administration	No	Yes
		1943–45	Independent State ("State of Burma")	?	Yes
Japan	Manchuria	1932–45	Independent State ("Manchukuo")	Yes	Yes
Japan	China	1940–45	Independent State ("Reorganized National Government of the Republic of China")	Yes	Yes
Japan	Java	1942–45	Military Administration	No	Yes
Japan	Philippines	1941–42	Military Administration	?	Yes
		1942–45	Independent State ("Second Philippine Republic")		
Japan	Thailand	1941–45	Independent State ("Kingdom of Thailand")	No	No

Source: Created by the author.

lesser development of trade union movements in the occupied countries and regions, Japanese military administrations dissolved these organizations and created new ones under state control in a more-or-less corporatist way, in some cases associated with single parties.[276] These dynamics were also present in the Japanese colonial rural world, notably in Korea, leading some scholars to underline how "corporatism can readily be combined with colonialism to produce what we term 'colonial corporatism'."[277] This policy (and its expansion all over the Japanese occupied areas) illustrate the clear diffusion of models and imposed transfers from Authoritarian Japan. Although there were different types of occupation in Asia, in many cases not creating occupation political regimes, social corporatism became an imperialist institutional tool for the societies under Japanese rule. As Gregg Huff has highlighted, the "second strand" of Japanese imperialism was to "convert Southeast Asians to a corporatist social behaviour like that in Japan, where individuals worked for the good of the state and accepted its benevolent rule ... In all countries except Thailand and Indochina, the Japanese set up a plethora of organisations to try to link individuals to the state and inculcate a spirit of work and sacrifice."[278]

The use of civilian, academic, and intellectual cadres for administration, and political, social, and propaganda institutions in occupied territories, marked the imperialist expansion of Japan in Asia. In comparison to other Axis powers, however, "from the beginning, the signals from within the Japanese imperial system were ambiguous and ambivalent, reflective on the one hand of the conservative inertia and provincialism of the Japanese military and bureaucracy, on the other of the revolutionary nature, challenge, and promise of the times."[279] In practice, the "think tanks" associated with the Japanese Army and Navy, regardless of the type of occupation, were instrumental in the ideological creation of a model of social organization "not meant to be colonial or harshly domineering. Far from it: 'organic difference' would lead to natural harmony – the harmony found in familial organization, where every member had its own function or role to fill. It sought to impose functionalist, corporatist, and family–state norms on the international sphere.

---

[276] See Paul H. Kratoska, "Labor mobilization in Japan and the Japanese empire," in Paul H. Kratoska, ed., *Asian Labor in the Wartime Japanese Empire. Unknown Histories*, London, Routledge, 2015, p. 12.

[277] Gi-Wook Shin and Do-Hyun Han, "Colonial corporatism: The rural revitalization campaign, 1932–1940," in Gi-Wook Shin and Michael Robinson, eds., *Colonial Modernity in Korea*, Cambridge, MA, Harvard University Asia Center, 1999, pp. 75–76. On fascism in colonial Korea, see Vladimir Tikhonov, "The controversies on fascism in colonial Korea in the early 1930s," *Modern Asian Studies*, 46, no. 4 (2012), pp. 975–1006.

[278] Huff, *World War II and Southeast Asia*, p. 18.

[279] Mark, *Japan's Occupation of Java in the Second World War*, p. 54.

The Japanese Empire would stand at the apex of the international system, as 'head' of this new 'familial community' of nations."[280]

To conclude: although not consolidated and in some cases only sketched, the dictatorships and the hybrid authoritarian occupation regimes under Axis rule represented the apogee of the Age of Fascism and the political institutions associated with it. This Element was therefore mainly concerned with institution-building in these dictatorships, trying to identify the design of their institutions, the segments of collaborationist political elites, diffusion processes, and conditionality of the models present. The "why" of the decision to allow their creation was compared with other options present and is certainly a research agenda that needs to be explored in more depth. In one way or another, though, part of the elite of these dictatorships, both in Europe and in Asia, accompanied the poles of the Axis in their military defeat regardless of their nature, be it fascist, conservative, radical right, or nationalist. As Ba Maw, President of the "State of Burma," wrote in his memoirs, the resistance movements "denounced the Japanese as fascists and called their movement an antifascist resistance."[281] Indeed, between stints at the German Castle of Sigmaringen or the Sugamo Prison in Tokyo, national and international trials and executions, most of this elite became associated with the Era of Fascism and its trial.[282] However, even if conjuncturally united by global antifascism in their punishment at the end of World War II, the personal and institutional legacies of Pétain, Quisling, and Monsignor Tiso (in Europe) and Chen Gongbo, Ba Maw, or José P. Laurel (in Asia) would nevertheless be quite different.[283]

---

[280] Yellen, *The Greater East Asia Co-Prosperity Sphere*, p. 84.
[281] Ba Maw, *Breakthrough in Burma*, p. 332.
[282] See, for Asia, Yuma Totani, *Justice in Asia and the Pacific Region, 1945–1952. Allied War Crimes Prosecutions*, New York, Cambridge University Press, 2015; Kerstin von Lingen, ed., *War Crimes Trials in the Wake of Decolonization and Cold War in Asia, 1945–1956: Justice in Time of Turmoil*, Cham, Palgrave, 2016.
[283] See for the legacies of Japanese Imperialism in East Asia during World War Two, Diana S. Kim, *Rethinking Colonial Legacies across Southeast Asia through the Lens of the Japanese Wartime Empire*, Cambridge, Cambridge University Press, 2025.

Select Bibliography

Bang, P. F., C. A. Bayly, and W. Scheidel, eds., *The Oxford World History of Empire*, vol. 2, Oxford, Oxford University Press, 2021.

Baranowski, S., *Nazi Empire*, Cambridge, Cambridge University Press, 2010.

Barrett, D. P. and L. N. Shyu, eds., *Chinese Collaboration with Japan, 1932–1945: The Limits of Accommodation*, Stanford, Stanford University Press, 2001.

Baruch, M. O., *Servir l'État Français: L'Administration en France de 1940 à 1944*, Paris, Fayard, 1997.

Basciani, A., *L'impero nei Balcani: L'occupazione italiana dell'Albania 1939–1943*, Roma, Viela, 2022.

Bauer, R., *The Construction of a National Socialist Europe during the Second World War: How the New Order Took Shape*, London, Routledge, 2020.

Benda, H. J., J. K. Irikura, and K. Kish, eds., *Japanese Military Administration in Indonesia: Selected Documents*, New Haven, CT, Southeast Asia Studies, Yale University, 1965.

Böhler, J. and R. Gerwarth, eds., *The Waffen-SS: A European History*, Oxford, Oxford University Press, 2017.

Boldorf, M. and T. Okazaki, eds., *Economies under Occupation: The Hegemony of Nazi Germany and Imperial Japan in World War II*, London, Routledge, 2015.

Bosworth, R. and J. Maiolo, eds., *The Cambridge History of the Second World War*, vol. 2, *Politics and Ideology*, Cambridge, Cambridge University Press, 2015.

Bourchier, D., *Illiberal Democracy in Indonesia: The Ideology of the Family State*, London, Routledge, 2015.

Brook, T., *Collaborating: Japanese Agents and Local Elites in Wartime China*, Cambridge, Harvard University Press, 2005.

Burgwyn, H. J., *Mussolini and the Salo` Republic, 1943–1945: The Failure of a Puppet Regime*, Cham, Palgrave, 2018.

Cattaruzza, M., *L'Italia e il confine orientale, 1866–2006*, Bologna, Il Mulino, 2007.

Cointet-Labrousse, M., *Vichy et Le Fascisme: Les Hommes, les Structures et les Pouvoirs*, Brussels, Editions Complexe, 1987.

Conway, M., *Collaboration in Belgium: Léon Degrelle and the Rexist Movement, 1940–1044*, New Haven, CT, Yale University Press, 1993.

Culver, A. A., *Glorify the Empire: Japanese Avant-Garde Propaganda in Manchukuo*, Vancouver, The University of British Columbia, 2013.

Dahl, H. F., *Quisling: A Study in Treachery*, Cambridge, Cambridge University Press, 1999.

Dallin, A., *German Rule in Russia, 1941–1945: A Study of Occupation Policies*, Boulder, CO, Westview Press, 1981.

Duara, P., *Sovereignty and Authenticity: Manchukuo and the East Asian Modern*, Lanham, MD, Rowman & Littlefield Publishers, 2003.

Edelstein, D. M., *Occupational Hazards: Success and Failure in Military Occupation*, Ithaca, NY, Cornell University Press, 2008.

Faure, C., *Le Project Culturel de Vichy*, Lyon, CNRS-Presses Universitaire de Lyon, 1989.

Fischer, B. J., *Albania at War*, West Lafayette, IN, Purdue University Press, 1999.

Fonzi, P., *Oltre i Confini: Le Occupazione Italiane Durante la Seconda Guerra Mondiale (1939–43)*, Florence, Le Monier, 2020.

Grant, W., J. Nekkers, and F. V. Waarden, eds., *Organising Business for War: Corporatist Economic Organisation during the Second World War*, Oxford, Berg, 1991.

Grillère, D., *L'Autre Occupation: L'Italie fasciste en France*, Paris, Nouveau Monde Édition, 2023.

Gross, J. T., *Polish Society under German Occupation: The General-gouvernement, 1939–1944*, Princeton, NJ, Princeton University Press, 1979.

Hedinger, D., *Die Achse Berlin-Rom-Tokio 1919–1946*, Munich, CH Beck, 2021.

Hirschfeld, G., *Nazi Rule and Dutch Collaboration: The Netherlands under German Occupation 1940–45*, Oxford, New York and Hamburg, Berg, 1988.

Hofmann, R., *The Fascist Effect: Japan and Italy, 1915–1952*, Ithaca, NY, and London, Cornell University Press, 2015.

Huff, G., *World War II and Southeast Asia: Economy and Society under Japanese Occupation*, Cambridge, Cambridge University Press, 2020.

Ishida, K., *Japan, Italy and the Road to the Tripartite Alliance*, London, Palgrave, 2019.

Janjetović, Z., *Collaboration and Fascism under the Nedić Regime*, Belgrade, Institute for Recent History of Serbia, 2018.

Kim, D. S., *Rethinking Colonial Legacies across Southeast Asia through the Lens of the Japanese Wartime Empire*, Cambridge, Cambridge University Press, 2025.

Klinkhammer, L., *L'occupazione tedesca in Italia: 1943–1945*, Turin, Bollati Boringhieri, 2016.

Kneuer, M. and T. Demmelhuber, eds., *Authoritarian Gravity Centers: A Cross-Regional Study of Authoritarian Promotion and Diffusion*, London, Routledge, 2021.

Kott, S. and K. K. Patel, eds., *Nazism across Borders: The Social Policies of the Third Reich and Their Global Appeal*, Oxford, Oxford University Press, 2018.

Kranjc, G. J., *To Walk with the Devil: Slovene Collaboration and Axis Occupation*, Toronto, The University of Toronto Press, 2013.

Kratoska, P. H., ed., *Asian Labor in the Wartime Japanese Empire: Unknown Histories*, London, Routledge, 2015.

Lehmann, S., R. Bohn, and U. Danker, eds., *Reichskommissariat Ostland: Tatort und Erinnerungsobjekt, Konstruktionen*, Paderborn, Ferdinand Schöningh, 2012.

Lemkin, R., *Axis Rule in Occupied Europe, Laws of Occupation, Analysis of Government, Proposals for Redress*, Washington, DC, Carnegie Endowment for International Peace, 1944.

Mark, E., *Japan's Occupation of Java in the Second World War: A Transnational History*, London, Bloomsbury, 2018.

Martin, B. G., *The Nazi-Fascist New Order for European Culture*, Cambridge, MA, Harvard University Press, 2016.

Matthienssen, S., *Japanese Pan-Asianism and the Philippines from the Late 19th Century to the End of World War II: Going to the Philippines Is Like Coming Home?*, Leiden, Brill, 2016.

Maw, B., *Breakthrough in Burma: Memoirs of a Revolution, 1939–1946*, New Haven, CT, Yale University Press, 1968.

Mazower, M., *Inside Hitler's Greece: The Experience of Occupation, 1941–44*, New Haven, CT, Yale University Press, 1993.

Mazower, M., *Hitler's Empire: Nazi Rule in Occupied Europe*, London, Allen Lane, 2008.

Mimura, J., *Planning for Empire: Reform Bureaucrats and the Japanese Wartime State*, Ithaca, NY: Cornell University Press, 2011.

Mitter, R., *The Manchurian Myth Nationalism, Resistance, and Collaboration in Modern China*, Berkeley, The University of California Press, 2000.

Morgan, P., *Hitler's Collaborators: Choosing between Bad and Worse in Nazi-occupied Western Europe*, Oxford, Oxford University Press, 2018.

Newman, J. P., *Yugoslavia in the Shadow of War*, Cambridge, Cambridge University Press, 2015.

Pinto, A. C., ed., *Corporatism and Fascism: The Corporatist Wave in Europe*, London, Routledge, 2017.

Pinto, A. C., ed., *An Authoritarian Third Way in the Era of Fascism: Diffusion, Models and Interactions in Europe and Latin America*, London, Routledge, 2022.

Pinto, A. C., and G. Adinolfi, eds., *Building Dictatorships under Axis Rule: War, Military Occupation and Political Regimes*, London, Routledge, 2025.

Prusin, A., *Serbia under the Swastika: A World War II Occupation*, Champaign, University of Illinois Press, 2017.

Reynolds, E. B., *Thailand and Japan's Southern Advance, 1940–1945*, New York, S. Martin's Press, 1994.

Rodogno, D., *Fascism's European Empire: Italian Occupation during the Second World War*, Cambridge, Cambridge University Press, 2006.

Sato, S., *War, Nationalism and Peasants Java under the Japanese Occupation 1942–1945*, Armonk, NY, M. E. Sharp, 1994.

Shin'ichi, Y., *Manchuria under Japanese Dominion*, Philadelphia, University of Pennsylvania Press, 2006.

Soutou, G.-H., *Europa! Les Projects Européens de L'Allemagne Nazie et L'Italie Fasciste*, Paris, Tallandier, 2021.

Steinberg, D. J., *Philippine Collaboration in World War II*, Ann Arbor, The University of Michigan Press, 1967.

Stirk, P. M. R., *The Politics of Military Occupation*, Edinburgh, Edinburgh University Press, 2009.

Šustrová, R., *Nations Apart: Czech Nationalism and Authoritarian Welfare under Nazi Rule*, Oxford, Oxford University Press, 2024.

Taylor, J. E., *Iconographies of Occupation: Visual Cultures in Wang Jingwei's China, 1939–1945*, Honolulu, University of Hawai'i Press, 2021.

Trager, F. N., ed., *Burma: Japanese Military Administration, Selected Documents, 1941–1945*, Philadelphia, The University of Pennsylvania Press, 1971.

Verney, S., *L'Indochine sous Vichy. Entre Révolution nationale, collaboration et identités nationales 1940–1945*, Paris, Riveneuve éditions, 2012.

Ward, J. M., *Priest, Politician, Collaborator: Jozef Tiso and the Making of Fascist Slovakia*, Ithaca, NY, and London, Cornell University Press, 2013.

Warmbrunn, W., *The Dutch under German Occupation, 1940–45*, Stanford, CA, Stanford University Press, 1963.

Warmbrunn, W., *The German Occupation of Belgium, 1940–1944*, New York, Peter Lang, 1993.

Yellen, J., *The Greater East Asia Co-Prosperity Sphere: When Total Empire Met Total War*, Ithaca, NY, Cornell University Press, 2019.

Young, L., *Japan's Total Empire: Manchuria and the Culture of Wartime Imperialism*, Berkeley, The University of California Press, 1998.

Zanasi, M., *Saving the Nation: Economic Modernity in Republican China*, Chicago, IL, University of Chicago Press, 2006.

Note: for a complete list of sources and bibliography cited, see the footnotes.

Acknowledgments

This Element was born out of a broader inquiry into the diffusion of authoritarian institutions in fascist-era dictatorships, and specially of the research project "Building Dictatorships under Axis Rule" that I have co-organized with Goffredo Adinolfi. I would like to thank the participants in that project, whose results have been published in the meantime and are quoted abundantly above, since I am developing here the main theoretical and empirical aspects of my introduction to that volume, and to the two reviewers. Preliminary versions of this research have been presented in the panel "Collaborationist Regimes" at the Conventions of the International Association for Comparative Fascist Studies (ComFas), Central European University, Vienna, in 2023; at the Autonomous University of Barcelona, in May 2025; and at the 2nd Military History Consortium Conference, Lisbon, in June 2025. All errors and shortcomings remain, of course, solely my own.

Cambridge Elements

The History and Politics of Fascism

Series Editors

Federico Finchelstein
The New School for Social Research

Federico Finchelstein is Professor of History at the New School for Social Research and Eugene Lang College in New York City. He is an expert on fascism, populism, and dictatorship. His previous books include *From Fascism to Populism in History* and *A Brief History of Fascist Lies.*

António Costa Pinto
University of Lisbon

António Costa Pinto is a Research Professor at the Institute of Social Sciences, University of Lisbon. He is a specialist in fascism, authoritarian politics, and political elites. He is the author and editor of multiple books on fascism, including (with Federico Finchelstein) *Authoritarianism and Corporatism in Europe and Latin America.*

Advisory Board

Giulia Albanese, *University of Padova*
Mabel Berezin, *Cornell University*
Maggie Clinton, *Middlebury College*
Sandra McGee Deutsch, *University of Texas, El Paso*
Aristotle Kallis, *Keele University*
Sven Reichardt, *University of Konstanz*
Angelo Ventrone, *University of Macerata*

About the Series

Cambridge Elements in the History and Politics of Fascism is a series that provides a platform for cutting-edge comparative research in the field of fascism studies. With a broad theoretical, empirical, geographic, and temporal scope, it will cover all regions of the world, and most importantly, search for new and innovative perspectives.

Cambridge Elements⁼

The History and Politics of Fascism

Elements in the Series

Populism and Fascism
Carlos de la Torre

The Rise of Mass Parties, Liberal Italy, and the Fascist Dawn (1919–1924)
Goffredo Adinolfi

Neo-Fascism and the Far Right in Brazil
Odilon Caldeira Neto

Intellectual Post-fascism?: The Conservative Revolution, Traditionalism and the Challenge to Liberal Democracy
Alberto Spektorowski

The Fascist Zenith: War and Dictatorship under Axis Rule
António Costa Pinto

A full series listing is available at: www.cambridge.org/CEHF

For EU product safety concerns, contact us at Calle de José Abascal, 56–1°,
28003 Madrid, Spain or eugpsr@cambridge.org.